Biblical Worldview I
Affirming a Biblical Worldview

BWVW 101

Dr. N. Troy Matthews
Liberty University

Biblical Worldview I: Affirming a Biblical Worldview – BWVW 101
Copyright © 2012 by Troy Matthews, Ed.D.

Scripture taken from the Holy Bible, King James Version, New Living Translation, New International Version.

All rights reserved. No part of this publication may be reproduced or transmitted in any form or by any means, electronic or mechanical, including photocopying, recording, or any information storage and retrieval system, without the written permission of the publisher.

Requests for permission to make copies of any part of the work should be mailed to:

Permissions Department
Academx Publishing Services, Inc.
P.O. Box 56527
Virginia Beach, VA 23456

Printed in the United States of America

ISBN-10: 1-60036-551-5
ISBN-13: 978-1-60036-551-5

TABLE OF CONTENTS

PART ONE: CRITICAL THINKING

    Chapter 1: Critical Thinking 1

PART TWO: DEFINING WORLDVIEW

    Chapter 2: Defining Worldview 13

PART THREE: DEFINING A BIBLICAL/CHRISTIAN WORLDVIEW

    Chapter 3: Defining a Biblical Worldview 21

    Chapter 4: Salvation 29

    Chapter 5: Biblical Ethic/Absolutes 35

    Chapter 6: Christian Liberties 45

PART FOUR: PROMINENT RELIGIOUS WORLDVIEWS

    Chapter 7: Hinduism 51

    Chapter 8: Buddhism 59

    Chapter 9: Islam 65

PART FIVE: PROMINENT PHILOSOPHICAL WORLDVIEWS

    Chapter 10: Relativism 73

    Chapter 11: Teleological Ethics 77

    Chapter 12: Determinism 83

    Chapter 13: Nihilism 89

    Chapter 14: Tolerance 93

BIBLIOGRAPHY: 97

Chapter One

CRITICAL THINKING
Affirming a Biblical Worldview

Proverbs 14:15 (NIV) - *A simple man believes anything but prudent man gives thoughts to his steps.*

Acts 17:11(NLT) - *And the people of Berea were more open-minded than those in Thessalonica, and they listened eagerly to Paul's message. They searched the Scriptures day after day to check up on Paul and Silas, to see if they were really teaching the truth.*

Colossians 2:8 (NLT) - *Don't let anyone lead you astray with empty philosophy and high-sounding nonsense that come from human thinking and from the evil powers of this world, and not from Christ.*

1 Peter 3:15 (NIV) - *But in your hearts set apart Christ as Lord. Always be prepared to give an answer to everyone who asks you to give the reason for the hope that you have. But do this with gentleness and respect . . .*

I. What is Critical Thinking?

A. It is recognizing and evaluating _____ and so-called _____.

B. It is reflecting on the meaning and significance of statements and ideas.

C. It tests the _____ of statements and ideas.

D. It is an approach to ideas for the purpose of deliberate consideration.

E. It is NOT:

1. Simply thinking negatively or looking to find faults and flaws as the term critical is often used.

2. A belief itself, rather it is a process whereby the validity of one's beliefs may be evaluated.

DEFINITION

"Critical thinking is a self-guided, self-disciplined process which directs individuals to think correctly about themselves and the world around them. It is an essential method that guides its adherents toward truth. It involves investigation, analysis and self-corrective decision making which provide a consistent and coherent way to solve problems and come to conclusions."

Weider & Gutierrez 2011, p19

II. Notable Terms Related to Critical Thinking

A. _____ – An opinion is any belief or conclusion about reality that is not based on absolute or indisputable knowledge, but rather seems valid or probable to the one who holds it. Opinions, therefore, are open to debate and questioning through critical thinking. Note: Opinions call for support with the use of evidence; facts on the other hand, are generally and unquestionably accepted as true by most people or the majority of people in a field of specialization, or authorities (those have spent significant time studying it and/or have significant firsthand experience).

B. _____ - In the formal sense, it is offering _____ to demonstrate the _____ of, and thus persuade others to accept, an opinion or conclusion one holds.

C. The LAW OF NON-CONTRADICTION

Foundational to getting at truth is recognizing the law of non-contradiction (LONC).

BIOGRAPHY

ARISTOTLE: "Ancient Greek philosopher Aristotle was born circa 384 B.C. in Stagira, Greece. When he turned 17, he enrolled in Plato's Academy. In 338, he began tutoring Alexander the Great. In 335, Aristotle founded his own school, the Lyceum, in Athens, where he spent most of the rest of his life studying, teaching and writing."

Aristotle, "together with Socrates and Plato, laid much of the groundwork for western philosophy".

Pertinent to critical thinking are his writings on logic, argumentation and ethics.

Aristotle. (2012). *Biography.com*. Retrieved 01:33, May 23, 2012 from http://www.biography.com/people/aristotle-9188415

"The same attribute cannot at the same time belong and not belong to the same subject in the same respect," and, "It is impossible that contrary attributes should belong at the same time to the same subject." Aristotle

Contradictory propositions about the same subject cannot both be true. That is, A cannot be non-A at the same time and from the same perspective.

The LONC is the basic law of logic that states:

If one statement is true; its _____ is false.

- Jerry Falwell the Founder and Chancellor of Liberty University in Lynchburg, VA
- Jerry Falwell is not the Founder and Chancellor of Liberty University in Lynchburg, VA

- The Creator God of the Bible exists
- The Creator God of the Bible does not exist
- Jesus Christ is the only savior of mankind
- Jesus Christ is not the only savior of mankind

No two propositions, which contain contrary claims, can both be true at the same time and in the _____.

III. Characteristics of Critical Thinkers

A. They constantly evaluate _____ attitudes, values and opinions. (They seek to ensure that their opinions are reasonable, logically sound and not based upon emotion <u>alone.</u>)

B. They understand that having _____ _____ to an opinion does not mean every opinion is _____, including their own.

C. They do not _____ to know what they do not know. (They are honest with themselves, and admit their shortcomings and ignorance to others.)

D. They do not blindly adhere to _____. (They do not hold to cherished viewpoints if they are shown to have been developed from faulty reasoning, or emotion. They do not automatically reject a competing opinion until the evidence is examined, and are willing to (re)examine and even revise their viewpoint if evidence seems to warrant it.)

E. They resist, and refuse to use, _____. (They do not succumb to appeals to self-indulgence, impulsiveness, and instant gratification. They also do not use these tactics on others.)

F. They seek clarification of _____. (They do not allow others to use ambiguous terms without having them defined, nor do they use terms without careful definition.)

G. They explore the _____ _____ of an issue. (Before beginning to formulate their opinions or committing to a course of action, they ask questions, challenge others viewpoints, and give all sides of an issue a fair hearing.)

H. They base their opinions and judgments on _____. (To the best of their ability they research issues to base judgments on the best available supporting evidence, not wishful thinking, hearsay, the popular viewpoint, or because a celebrity figure believes and/or endorses it.)

I. They are _____ to _____ from the experiences of others. (They admit that they cannot possibly know everything, and are therefore open to competing opinions and viewpoints to gain insights into the issues.)

J. They look for common _____ in arguments. (They educate themselves regarding the logical fallacies that prevail in peoples' thinking and argumentation to avoid being persuaded by them, or using them themselves in their speaking and writing.)

K. They avoid barriers that impede Critical Thinking
   1. Human Limitations: Applies to everyone, although in different ways and degrees.
   2. Use of Language: The means by which words fail to communicate truth.
   3. Use of Faulty Argumentation and Logic: Logical Fallacies.

(Note: Some barriers are unintentional in nature while others may be manipulative and planned).

CRITICAL THINKING

"Critical thinking is more than just thinking critically in the sense of criticizing others' thoughts, or our own, by finding one or more of the three things that can go wrong with thoughts: ambiguities, falsehoods, or fallacies. Critical thinking means judgment and evaluation but it does not mean only negative evaluation.

Another word for "critical thinking" is "logical thinking." This is a high and holy thing, in fact a very Christian thing because the ultimate foundation of logic is the Logos, the eternal Mind or Reason or Inner Word of God, which John's Gospel identifies as the pre-incarnate Christ. The human art and science of logic is the instrument that teaches us to rightly order and structure our thoughts, as a means to the end of thought, which is truth."

Peter Kreeft –" Critical Thinking for Christians"http://www.catholicculture.org/culture/library/view.cfm?recnum=9243 July, 2012

Barrier to Critical Thinking	Barrier Described	Example	How to Avoid this Barrier
Human Limitations			
Selective thinking	The process whereby one tends to notice and look for what confirms one's beliefs, and to ignore, not look for, what contradicts one's beliefs.	If one believes that more murders occur during a full moon, then one will tend to take notice of murders that occur during a full moon and tend not to take notice of murders that occur at other times.	Objectively evaluate all relevant information and sides of an issue before passing judgment.
Ignorance	The lack of essential background knowledge or information on a subject prior to making a judgment.	One may be convinced a "Magician" has the power to levitate objects, but does not see the thin wire attached to them.	Perform appropriate research on multiple sides of issues to obtain all pertinent evidence, before reaching conclusions.
Senses	Being unaware the limitations of our senses that can lead to misconceptions about reality.	Looking up at the stars at night and perceiving they are as close as the moon and planets.	Recognize that "seeing is not always believing." Know when & how to verify your observations with other sources.
Personal Biases & Prejudices	We each have personal biases and prejudices, resulting from our own unique life experiences and worldview, which make it difficult to remain objective and think critically.	Some people are biased against claims made by the Bible because it is not a science book or science because it is not mentioned in the Bible.	Resist your own biases by focusing on the facts, their sources, and the reasoning in support of arguments.
Physical & Emotional	Stress, fatigue, drugs, and related hindrances can severely affect our ability to think clearly and critically.	Air traffic controllers often have difficulty making good judgments after long hours on duty	Restrain from making critical decisions when extremely exhausted or stressed.
Testimonial Statements	Relying on the testimonies and vivid anecdotes of others to substantiate one's own beliefs.	Dramatic stories of Bigfoot sightings do not prove the existence of Bigfoot.	Resist making judgments based on testimonies alone.

Chapter One - Critical Thinking

Barrier to Critical Thinking	Barrier Described	Example	How to Avoid this Barrier
Use of Language			
Ambiguity	A word or expression that can be understood in more than one way.	John says that he is a Christian. What does that mean and how does he define "Christian."	Clarify terms and avoid making judgments if the terms remain ambiguous.
Assuring Expressions	Using expressions that disarm you from questioning the validity of an argument.	Expressions such as "As everyone knows…", and "Common sense tells us that…"	Disregard assuring expressions and instead focus on facts & reasoning that support arguments.
Doublespeak Euphemisms	The use of inoffensive words or expressions to mislead, disarm, or deceive us about unpleasant realities.	Referring to a policy of mass murder as "ethnic cleansing" or the inadvertent killing of innocent people as "collateral damage."	Look beyond the emotional content and recognize the factual content of euphemistic words and expressions.
Judgmental Words	Stating opinions as though they were facts, so the audience does not have to "bother" judging for themselves.	The President took justifiable pride in signing the peace treaty.	Distinguish what is fact from what is opinion in any statement or argument.
Meaningless Comparisons	Language that implies that something is superior but retreats from that view.	An ad that claims a battery lasts "up to" 30% longer, but does not say it will last 30% longer, and if it did, longer than what?	Avoid making judgments if it is not exactly clear what is being compared.
Vagueness	Language which is less precise than the context requires.	If someone needs to be paid back tomorrow, and the borrower says "I'll pay you back soon", the borrower's response was too vague.	Be aware of the consequences of imprecise claims based on vagueness.

Chapter One - Critical Thinking

Barrier to Critical Thinking	Barrier Described	Example	How to Avoid this Barrier
Faulty Argumentation or Logic			
Superstition	Erroneous perception of the connections between unrelated events.	Irrationally believing that how one wears their hat while watching a football game can influence the score.	Recognize the difference between cause & effect versus unrelated coincidence.
See below, "Logical Fallacies" as explained and described.			

Charts based on *A Practical Guide to Critical Thinking* by Greg R. Haskins.

A FEW EXAMPLES OF LOGICAL FALLACIES TO BE AWARE OF

DEFINITION

LOGICAL FALLACIES: The use of Faulty Argumentation -
In rhetoric, a fallacy is simply any error, whether intentional or unintentional, in reasoning. Think of them as the counterfeits of arguments.

1. _____ – Concluding that an effect has only one cause when it is really the result of multiple causes.

   Reasoning Formula:

   1. The result R was caused by A.
   2. Eliminate A and your will eliminate the result R.
   Example:

2. _____ - Making a judgment on the basis of one or even a few samples.

   Reasoning Formula:

   1. Sample S, which is too small, is taken from population P.
   2. Conclusion C is drawn about Population P based on S.

   Example:

Chapter One - Critical Thinking

3. _____ - (Stereotyping) - Making a judgment about an entire Group based on behavior, mostly undesirable, of a few from that group.

   Reasoning Formula:

   1. (Same as Hasty Conclusion) Sample S, which is too small, is taken from population P.
   2. Conclusion C is drawn about Population P based on S.

   Example:

4. _____ - Arguing on the basis of a comparison of unrelated things.

   Reasoning Formula:

   1. x is similar to y.
   2. x is P.
   3. Therefore, y is P.

   Example:

5. _____ - Arguing against an action on the unsupported assertion that it will inevitably lead to a much worse condition.

   Reasoning Formula:

   1. If A happens, then by a gradual series of small steps through B, C,…, X, Y, eventually Z will happen, too.
   2. Z should not happen.
   3. Therefore, A should not happen, either.

   Example:

6. _____ - Stating a general principle and then applying it in a specific case as though it were a universal rule.

   Reasoning Formula:

   1. Xs are normally Ys.
   2. A is an X. (Where A is abnormal.)
   3. Therefore, A is a Y.

   Example:

7. _____ (Lit. "To the man") - Seeking to discredit a person's argument by attacking their personal character, origin, associations, etc.

Reasoning Formula:

1. Person A makes claim X.
2. Person B makes an attack on person A.
3. Therefore A's claim is false.

Example:

8. _____ - Appealing to the opinion of a person who agrees with yours because they are generally respected by the audience, but have no real authority on the topic at hand.

Reasoning Formula:

1. Person A is (claimed to be) an authority on subject S.
2. Person A makes claim C about subject S.
3. Therefore, C is true.

Example:

9. _____ - Claiming that something is true simply because it cannot be disproved, or that something is untrue because it cannot be proved.

Reasoning Formula:

1. There is no evidence against P. Therefore, P.
2. There is no evidence for p. Therefore, not-p.

Example:

10. _____ - Justifying a course of action because "everyone is doing it."

Reasoning Formula:

1. Person P is pressured by his/her peers or threatened with rejection.
2. Therefore person P claims the proposed X whether convinced or not.

Example:

11. _____ - Concluding about the way things ought to be simply on the basis of how things are or are assumed to be.

   Reasoning Formula:

   1. The status S is how it is.
   2. Therefore, S is correct

   Example:

12. _____ - Looking only for things that support our current ideas, and ignoring evidence that does not.

   Reasoning Formula:

   1. Person P seeks to prove claim X.
   2. P refuses to seek Y or ignores evidence Y if it opposes X.

   Example:

13. _____ - Oversimplifying a complex issue to make it appear that only two alternatives are possible.

   Reasoning Formula:

   1. Either claim X is true or claim Y is true (when there may be more possibilities. A,B,C).
   2. Claim Y is false.
   3. Therefore claim X is true.

   Example:

14. _____ - Raising an irrelevant issue to divert attention from the primary issue.

   Reasoning Formula:

   1. Topic A is under discussion.
   2. Topic B is introduced under the guise of being relevant to topic A (when topic B is actually not relevant to topic A).
   3. Topic A is abandoned.

   Example:

15. _____ - The <u>Straw Man</u> fallacy is committed when <u>a person</u> simply ignores a person's actual position and substitutes a distorted, exaggerated or misrepresented version of that position.

Reasoning Formula

1. Person A has position X.
2. Person B presents position Y   (which is a distorted version of X).
3. Person B attacks position Y.
4. Therefore X is false/incorrect/flawed.

Example:

(These are but a sampling of the Logical Fallacies that can be investigated. Further investigation and study will identify many others along with their variations.)

Informal Logical Fallacies – Example sheet

(For practice identify the fallacies. The answers are at the bottom of the page)

1. Argument
"We need to round up every single person of Middle Eastern descent and ship them all back to their own country. If we are going to restore any sense of security to this great land, we need to take drastic measures and get rid of all these terrorists . . . and anyone who looks like one." _____

2. Argument
"Everyone ought to be drinking Green Tea. The Chinese drink it all the time and they do not have near the incidents of heart disease that we do in the U.S. Further, most Chinese men live at least twenty more years than the average American male."
_____

3. Argument
"Here is my opponent, speaking to you of the values of abstinence and abstinence education when everyone knows she had a child out of wedlock while a teenager herself!"
_____

4. Argument
"The holocaust was a terrible misfortune, but while 6,000, 000 Jews were killed during the Holocaust, there are over 600 million chickens killed every year just to satisfy our hunger for flesh!" _____

5. Argument
"Hanes must be the best underwear on the market, you know they're Michael Jordan's favorites." _____

6. Argument
"I know that God exists because no atheist, no matter how clever, has ever provided evidence to the contrary." _____

7. Argument
"I cannot believe that the US, as civilized as it is, still allows the death penalty. Most other countries have already made capital punishment unlawful. How can the US continue this barbaric practice?" _____

8. Argument
"Because humans can be shown to do everything, ultimately, for their own benefit, we should always and only do that which is in our best interest."
_____

9. Argument
<u>Person A</u>: It has not been proven that the unborn are not persons, shouldn't we therefore err on the side of life? Has it never occurred that we just may be sanctioning murder?
<u>Person B</u>: Well, speaking of death, if, as my opponent desires, abortion were 'illegal except to save the woman's life,' women will resort to "back-alley" abortions again, which are very unsafe and often deadly. _____

10. Argument
"Did you see that child sipping wine? I can't believe these parents who allow this. Today it's few sips of wine, in ten years, it's another problem alcoholic, driving drunk on the road, killing our loved ones!" _____

11. Argument
"Gay rights are the issue of greatest importance at this time in our nation. It's the last oppression. The US must take this step in ending oppression, just like it did when it outlawed slavery and established civil rights for its black citizens."
_____

12. Argument
"Affirmative action means one thing, injustice. As we continue to set quotas that keep qualified white males from getting jobs, we are promoting reverse discrimination. Face it, if you are not against affirmative action, you are for injustice."
_____

13. Argument
" She will never make it in college she made C's and D's in High School"
_____

14. Argument
" As Americans we have believe in 'freedom of the press' therefore, reporters should not be hindered from reporting our troops movements in the war zone."
_____

ANSWERS:
1) Overgeneralization/Stereotyping 2) Oversimplification   3) Ad Hominen
4) False Analogy 5) Appeal to False Authority   6) Appeal to Ignorance
7) Bandwagon   8) Is/Ought - Naturalistic Fallacy   9) Red Herring
10) Slippery Slope   11) False Analogy   12) False Dilemma
13) Hasty Conclusion   14) Sweeping Generalization

Chapter Two

WORLDVIEW

Affirming a Biblical Worldview

Genesis 1:1(KJV) - *In the beginning God created the heaven and the earth.*

Job 14:14(KJV) - *If a man die, shall he live [again]? all the days of my appointed time will I wait, till my change come.*

Romans 12:1-2 (KJV) - *I beseech you therefore, brethren, by the mercies of God, that ye present your bodies a living sacrifice, holy, acceptable unto God, [which is] your reasonable service. And be not conformed to this world: but ye transformed by the renewing of your mind, that ye may prove what [is] that good, and acceptable, and perfect, will of God.*

Acts 28 1-6 – (Notice the reaction of the people based upon their worldview.)

What is a Worldview?

Do I have a worldview?

DEFINITION

Worldview:
- The overall perspective from which one sees and interprets the world.

The American Heritage® Dictionary of the English Language, Fourth Edition copyright ©2000 by Houghton Mifflin Company

I. What a Worldview is NOT.

A. It is _____ merely our _____ of the world.

    i.e., "Our society is really sinful."

    - Our <u>perception</u> or <u>opinion</u> is not our worldview but rather it is the result of our worldview

B. It is not limited to those who study _____.

C. A worldview does NOT determine _____. (we will look at this further

II. What is a Worldview?

A. It is the basis for your moral _____ _____.

Chapter Two – Defining Worldview

B. A set of _____ by which we order our lives and that determine our religious, ethical and social beliefs, values and practices.

DEFINITION

- **Presuppose** - To believe or suppose in advance. To require or involve necessarily as an antecedent condition. See Synonyms at presume.
- **Presupposition** - the act of presupposing; a supposition made prior to having knowledge (as for the purpose of argument)
- A collection of beliefs about life and the universe held by an individual or a group.

The American Heritage® Dictionary of the English Language, Fourth Edition copyright ©2000 by Houghton Mifflin

- "A world view is a set of presuppositions (assumptions which may be true, partially true or entirely false) which we hold (consciously **or subconsciously, consistently or inconsistently) about the basic make-up of our world.**"

James W. Sire *The Universe Next Door*, (Intervarsity, 1988)

What are <u>presuppositions</u>?

1. Any ideas or concepts which we _____ as being "_____-_____" truths about reality and upon which we _____ all of our other beliefs, values and convictions.

2. Presuppositions cannot be _____ to be true with scientific certainty. While they cannot be proven beyond a "_____ doubt," they must be proven beyond a "_____ doubt."

Who has <u>presuppositions</u>? _____.
So who has a <u>worldview</u>? _____.

3. The relationship between FAITH and PRESUPPOSITIONS.
Faith is taking a step in the direction of the presuppositions that best explain the _____ (facts, data), yet it is a step _____ the evidence. (Hebrews 11:1, 6)

Who lives by faith? _____.

Since no one can escape having presuppositions, and living by faith, the issue becomes one of what presuppositions are

SCRIPTURE

Hebrews 11:1 (ESV) Now faith is the assurance of things hoped for, the conviction of things not seen.

Chapter Two – Defining Worldview

_____ to hold, or have faith in, because they best explain the facts?

Important: Your worldview choice is not a matter of choosing bias over non-bias, everyone is biased. The issue is that of *"which bias is the best bias with which to be biased."* (Ken Ham, Answers in Genesis)

C. Simply put: A "Worldview" is: _____
_____ .

- "It is simply the sum total of our beliefs about the world, the "big picture" that directs our daily decisions and actions."
  Charles Colson & Nancy Pearcey, *How Shall We Live* (Tyndale House, 1999)
- It's like looking through colored glasses or lenses. What we see is impacted by the tint of the lens.
- "A worldview, whether Christian or secular, is the unifying perspective from which we organize our thinking about life, death, art, science, faith, learning, work, money, values, and morals. A worldview is our underlying philosophy of life."
  Ken Hemphill, *Life Answers*, (Lifeway Press, 1993)

Important note: Although everyone has a worldview already, most people have not thought about it and its implications. That is, they have a worldview by _____ (passive absorption of what parents, pastors, peers and other influences have communicated) and not through _____ (careful personal consideration before reaching a conclusion). Consequently, they hold contradictory ideas without even realizing it. As Christians this is problematic, because we tend to have ideas about the world and how to live in it that are not consistent with the worldview of the Bible, God's Word.

What external forces influence our personal worldview?

Chapter Two – Defining Worldview

III. Three Major Worldviews

A. _____ – The only reality exists in the natural realm

Examples: *Secular Humanism* - Man is the central focus of decision making. *Postmodernism* - No truth exists outside of human experience (thus no god), only because of it. Truth (and what a society believes about god) is a "social construct" and is thus subject to change as human need and interest changes. *Atheism* – God does not exist

B. _____ - God and the world are the same thing.

Examples: *Eastern religions, Christian Science, The New Age movement,* etc.

C. _____ – God exists, was the creator of the world, and is personally and intimately involved with His creation. God operates through natural law but can and does intervene in the affairs of mankind.

Examples: *Christianity, Judaism, and Islam*

AMERICA'S CULTURAL WORLDVIEW

While we have noted that each individual has a personal worldview, we must also acknowledge that society reflects its own worldview. Here in America for example the dominant ideologies that pervade our societal worldview would include materialism, subjectivism, hedonism, and pragmatism.

A._____:
- Philosophical concept:
- Social application: A society devoid of absolute Truth, and no spiritual anchor. Seeking satisfaction and meaning in possessions.

B. _____:
- Philosophical concept: There is no absolute Truth.
- Social application: "Everyone is entitled to their opinion." Feelings become authoritative! Moral and social chaos ensues, for there are no absolutes of right and wrong.

C. _____:
- Philosophical concept:
- Social application: *Pursuit of pleasure, comfort, safety and security in human terms. All struggle and pain is defined as evil. Delayed gratification is considered to be evil.* "If it feels good, do it!"

D. _____:
- Philosophical concept:
- Social application: The end justifies the means. Focus upon intentions rather than upon right and wrong. If "intentions" are good, it does not matter if what we are doing is wrong, according to this viewpoint.

IV. Five Key Questions that Define your Worldview

The way in which you answer the following questions will serve well to reveal your worldview.

1. The question of _____ -

"How did life begin in the first place?" "Where did I come from?"

2. The question of _____ -

"What does it mean to be a human?" "Am I more important than animals?"

3. The question of _____ (purpose)-

"Why are we here?" "Why am I here?"

4. The question of _____ (ethics)-

"What is meant by right and wrong?" "How should I live?"

5. The question of _____ -

"Is there life after death?" "What will happen to me when I die?" "Will I have to answer for the choices I made and how I lived my life?"

I Per 3:15 (ESV) But in your hearts honor Christ the Lord as holy, always being prepared to make a defense to anyone who asks you for a reason for the hope that is in you; yet do it with gentleness and respect,
Colossians 2:6-7 (ESV) Therefore, as you received Christ Jesus the Lord, so walk in him, (7) rooted and built up in him and established in the faith, just as you were taught, abounding in thanksgiving.

"Christians must understand the clash of worldviews that is changing American Society. And we must stand ready to respond as people grow disillusioned with false beliefs and values and as they begin to seek real answers. We must know not only what our worldview is and why we believe it but also how to defend it. We must also have some understanding of the opposing worldviews and why people believe them. Only then can we present the gospel in language that can be understood. Only then can we defend truth in a way that is winsome and persuasive"

(Colson & Pearcey 1999, p.26)

Question: If asked… could you defend your faith, your worldview?

Questions: What would you say if an individual asked you why you believe that the Bible is the Word of God or that Jesus was the Son of God? Do we have an answer? What evidence or arguments might we use?

Chapter Two – Defining Worldview

Worldview – R.C Sproul (video)

As you view the video answer the following:

1. What is a worldview?

2. What is the ultimate division in terms of systems or worldviews?

3. Define:

    a. Theocentric –

    b. Anthropocentric –

4. What is "syncretism"?

5. At what "point" is the conflict between the two systems most clearly seen?

6. What is Nihilism -

Chapter Three

BIBLICAL WORLDVIEW
Affirming a Biblical Worldview

Genesis 1:1(KJV) - *In the beginning God created the heaven and the earth.*

John 14:6(KJV) - *Jesus said to him, "I am the way, and the truth, and the life. No one comes to the Father except through me.*

Romans 12:1-2 (KJV) - *I beseech you therefore, brethren, by the mercies of God, that ye present your bodies a living sacrifice, holy, acceptable unto God, [which is] your reasonable service. And be not conformed to this world: but be ye transformed by the renewing of your mind, that ye may prove what [is] that good, and acceptable, and perfect, will of God.*

> "A world view is a set of presuppositions (assumptions which may be true, partially true or **entirely false) which we hold (consciously or subconsciously, consistently or inconsistently)** about the basic make-up of our world."
>
> James W. Sire *The Universe Next Door*, (Intervarsity, 1988)

I. Five Key Questions that Define your Worldview

1) **The question of _____**

    Genesis 1:1 (NKJV) - *In the beginning God created the heavens and the earth.*

    Genesis 1:26-27 (NKJV) - *Then God said, "Let Us make man in Our image, according to Our likeness; let them have dominion over the fish of the sea, over the birds of the air, and over the cattle, over all the earth and over every creeping thing that creeps on the earth." So God created man in His own image; in the image of God He created him; male and female He created them.*

    "How did life begin in the first place?"
    "Where did I come from?"

2) **The question of _____**

    Genesis 1:27-28 (NKJV) - *So God created man in His own image; in the image of God He created him; male and female He created them. Then God blessed them, and God* said to them, "Be fruitful and multiply; fill the earth and subdue it; have dominion over the fish of the sea, over the birds of the air, and over every living thing that moves on the earth."

Romans 3:23 (NIV) - *for all have sinned and fall short of the glory of God*

"What does it mean to be a human?"
"Am I more important than animals?"

3) **The question of _____ (purpose)**

Matthew 22:37-40 (ESV) - *And he said to him, "You shall love the Lord your God with all your heart and with all your soul and with all your mind. This is the great and first commandment. And a second is like it: You shall love your neighbor as yourself. On these two commandments depend all the Law and the Prophets."*

Matthew 28:18-20 (NIV) *Then Jesus came to them and said, "All authority in heaven and on earth has been given to me. Therefore go and make disciples of all nations, baptizing them in the name of the Father and of the Son and of the Holy Spirit, and teaching them to obey everything I have commanded you. And surely I am with you always, to the very end of the age."*

"Why are we here?"
"Why am I here?"

 **THINKING**

Question: How do we know what is "right"?
Question: What is the source of moral truth?
(We will discuss this later)

4) **The question of _____ (ethics)**

Matthew 22:37-40 (see verses above)

"What is meant by right and wrong?"
"How should I live?"

5) **The question of _____**

Hebrews 9:27-28 (ESV) - *And just as it is appointed for man to die once, and after that comes judgment...*

Philippians 1:21, 23 (NIV) - *For to me, to live is Christ and to die is gain. I am torn between the two: I desire to depart and be with Christ, which is better by far.*

Revelation 20:11-15 (NET) - *Then I saw a large white throne and the one who was seated on it; the earth and the heaven fled from his presence, and no place was found for them. And I saw the dead, the great and the small, standing before the throne. Then books were opened, and another book was opened – the book of life. So the dead were judged by what was written in the books, according to their deeds.*

"Is there life after death?"
"What will happen to me when I die?"
"Will I have to answer for how I lived my life?"

III. The Basis of a Biblical Worldview

A. _____ – (Genesis 1:1)

B. God has revealed _____ to mankind – (Hebrews 1:1-2)

C. _____ is God's son who is the redeemer of the world – (John 3:16)

D. The Bible is God's _____ – (II Tim. 3:16; II Peter 1:20-21)

E. Christians are to follow the teachings of the _____ (II Tim. 3:16-17; I Peter 1:16)

> **SCRIPTURE**
>
> **II. Timothy 3:16-17** (KJV)
> All scripture [is] given by inspiration of God, and [is] profitable for doctrine, for reproof, for correction, for instruction in righteousness. (v.17) That the man of God may be perfect, thoroughly furnished unto all good works.

"Christians must understand the clash of worldviews that is changing the face of American Society

IV. Christians do not Seriously Consider their Worldview.

Because of this many Christians:

A. Have an understanding of life that is _____ .

B. Use the _____ to _____ answer certain questions while adopting the world's philosophies for others.

C. Have a Biblical faith that may give hope for issues of eternity but it is seemingly useless in practical matters such as:

i. _____
ii. _____
iii. _____
iv. _____
v.

"... the most important thing we can communicate to a postmodern world is a coherent and compelling Christian worldview. We have the challenge and privilege of inviting people to occupy with us a biblical way of answering the questions of who made us, why we exist, how we are to live, and what happens when we die."

    David W. Henderson, *Culture Shift: Communicating God's Truth to our Changing World.* (Baker Books, 1998.)

V. Why We Need a Worldview Based Upon the Bible

    (by Ken Hemphill - Lifeway Press, 1993)

1. A worldview helps us integrate biblical principles with _____.(the "glasses, the"filter")

2. A clear understanding of the biblical worldview provides _____ for and gives substance to our faith. *(Luke 6:46-49)*

3. A clear understanding of our worldview is essential because of an overt challenge from the secular world. *(Eph 4:14)*

4. A coherent worldview gives us a more effective _____ in the marketplace. *(I Peter 3:15)*

5. A clear understanding of the Christian worldview is essential because the _____ has become our _____. *(Titus 1:9)*

6. We must clearly understand the Christian worldview because it is commanded in Scripture. *(Col 2:6-7,* II Tim. 3:16-17; I Peter 1:16)

 **SCRIPTURE**

I Per 3:15 (ESV) But in your hearts honor Christ the Lord as holy, always being prepared to make a defense to anyone who asks you for a reason for the hope that is in you; yet do it with gentleness and respect,

Colossians 2:6-8 (ESV) Therefore, as you received Christ Jesus the Lord, so walk in him, (7) rooted and built up in him and established in the faith, just as you were taught, abounding in thanksgiving. (8) See to it that no one takes you captive by philosophy and empty deceit, according to human tradition, according to the elemental spirits of the world, and not according to Christ.

> "A biblical worldview is foundational for accurately interpreting reality in a manner that coincides with God's revealed truths." – Robert Velarde, *What Einstein's Brain Can Teach Us About Worldviews,* (www.trueu.org, 2005).

Our worldview must have a firm foundation in the Bible if we are to establish consistent Biblical standards.

The Worldview Triangle/Pyramid

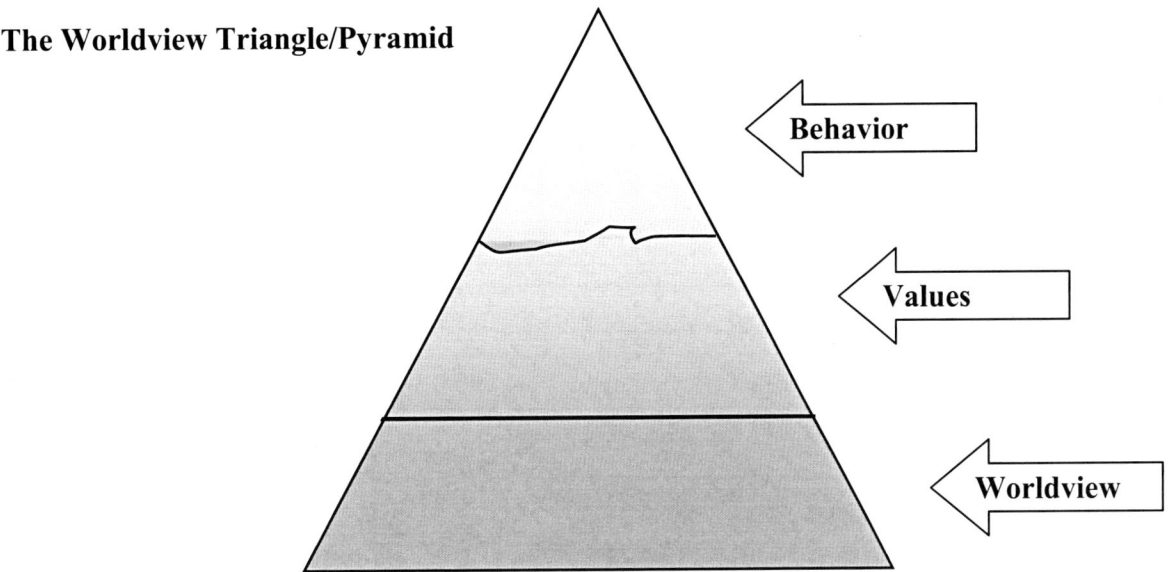

Our behavior is shaped by our values, which are ultimately built upon the foundation of our worldview

McDowell, Josh. & Bob Hostetler. *Beyond Belief to Conviction.* (Wheaton, IL; Tyndale House, 2002)

"Most discussions about Christian worldview formation correctly presuppose that students come to our colleges and universities as individuals whose minds need to be cultivated to think about their lives and chosen disciplines. However, there seems to be little emphasis on the fact that our students come to us possessing a variety of worldviews already. Their worldviews are the products of countless agents acting on them – peers, their culture, their particular denominational heritage, their own spiritual journey, their education to date…. Thus when we endeavor to communicate a Christian worldview, we are not starting with open plots ready for cultivation; we are starting with densely populated intellectual ground with various worldviews firmly entrenched and others competing for space.

(Kanitz, Lori. *Improving Christian Worldview Pedagogy: Going Beyond Mere Christianity.* Christian Higher Education, Taylor Francis Inc. 2005

The values of thinking through (cultivating) your worldview.
(Or why be concerned about worldview?)

- Helps you to clarify the important issues and ideas of life.
- Helps you see how the "bits and pieces" fit into the "bigger picture."
- Helps you appreciate the "beauty" of the Christian worldview as a coherent, adequate and relevant system of thought.
- Helps you identify and resist non- and anti-Christian "winds of doctrine." (Ephesians 4:14)
- Helps you to logically make a case for your beliefs to others. (1 Peter 3:15)
- Helps you to intelligently challenge others to explain and defend their belief systems (both Christians and non-Christians – everyone has to do apologetics!)
- Prepares you to give the answers to the questions people are really concerned about. (Who am I? Why am I here? Where did all this come from? Why do we suffer? How can I know there's a God? Etc.)
- Equips you to engage your culture more intelligently and effectively as you focus on the root causes of the "issues" rather than just the issues themselves.

THINKING

Question: what does it mean to be "holy"?

Question: What is your/ our standard for holiness?

Question: How does this standard align with the principles found within the Word of God?

Romans 12:1-2 (KJV) - *I beseech you therefore, brethren, by the mercies of God, that ye present your bodies a living sacrifice, <u>holy</u>, acceptable unto God, [which is] your reasonable service. And be not conformed to this world: but be ye transformed by the renewing of your mind, that ye may prove what [is] that good, and acceptable, and perfect, will of God.*

Chapter Three – Biblical Worldview

Worldview Review
(Comparative Chart of Naturalism and Biblical Theism)

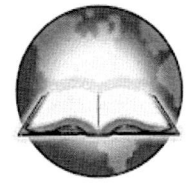

Important Note: These are obviously not the definite outcomes of either one of these worldviews. That is, the naturalist or secularist will not hold to all the viewpoints on the left column. And some who claim biblical theism will not consistently hold to every point in the right column. Both theists and non-theists inconsistently "borrow" from the other's worldview, often without realizing it, and usually for convenience sake. What these represent are the logical consequences of these primary belief systems. As biblical theists, we should seek to be more and more consistent with the right column when we think about and do ethics. And we must be able to show the naturalist/secularist the logical outcomes of his or her starting point.

Naturalism (Humanism, Secularism, Postmodernism)	Biblical Theism
God <u>DOES NOT</u> exist (Humanism/Materialism) or God's existence is <u>IRRELEVANT</u> to human life (Secularism).	A <u>PERSONAL</u> God exists as Creator, Sustainer, and Ruler of all. (Exodus 20:11, Nehemiah 9:6, Psalm 33:6)
<u>ANTHROPO</u>centric	<u>THEO</u>centric (1 Corinthians 10:31)
Humans are <u>ACCIDENTAL</u> products of chance <u>EVOLUTION</u> with no ultimate <u>PURPOSE</u> for being	Humans are <u>SPECIAL</u> creations <u>DESIGNED</u> by God to glorify Him and reflect His nature (Genesis 1:26-27, 2:7, Revelation 4:11)
Human life has <u>EXTRINSIC (CONDITIONAL)</u> value	Human life has <u>INTRINSIC (UNCONDITIONAL)</u> value (Genesis 1:27, 9:6, Psalm 8:4-5, Mark 8:36-37, James 3:9)
<u>QUALITY</u> of life	<u>SANCTITY</u> of life (Isaiah 46:3-4)
Man is <u>A SELF DETERMINED SOVEREIGN</u>	Man is <u>A SUBMISSIVE STEWARD</u> (Genesis 1:28 2:15, Psalm 8:6-8)
Human <u>AUTONOMY</u>	Divine <u>AUTHORITY</u> (Genesis 2:16-17, Isaiah 33:22)
Moral knowledge through unaided human <u>REASON</u>	Moral knowledge through divine <u>REVELATION</u> and reason (Proverbs 20:27, Romans 2:14,15, 2 Timothy 3:16,)

Chapter Three – Biblical Worldview

Naturalism (Humanism, Secularism, Postmodernism)	Biblical Theism
All moral truth originates in and is **DEPENDENT** upon human experience (**REALTIVE/SUBJECTIVE**)	Some moral truth is **OUTSIDE OF** and **INDEPENDENT** from human experience (**ABSOLUTE/OBJECTIVE**)
Ethical Emphasis: **TELEOLOGICAL** *"The ends JUSTIFY the means"*	Ethical Emphasis: **DEONTOLOGICAL** *"The ends and means must be JUST"*
Man **CONTROLS** and **MANIPULATES** nature according to **HUMAN WISH**.	Man **COOPERATES** with and **MAINTAINS** creation according to **DIVINE WILL** ("Cultural Mandate" Genesis 1:26-28)
TECHNOLOGY (ability) determines **MORALITY**	**MORALITY** limits **TECHNOLOGY** (can does not equal should)
SUFFERING is senseless	Suffering has **VALUE** (Romans 5:3-4, James 1:2-4)
Right to **DIE**	Responsibility to respect **LIFE** (including my own) (Exodus 20:13, Romans 13:8-10)
Death **ENDS** all **SUFFERING**	Death may begin **ENDLESS SUFFERING** (Revelation 20:11-15)
At death: **NO ACCOUNTABILITY** for what we believed and how we behaved.	At death: **ACCOUNTABILITY** for what we believed and how we behaved (Ecclesiastes 11:9, 12:14, Matthew 12:36, Hebrews 9:27)

"I believe in Christianity like I believe that the sun has risen, not only because I can see it, but by it I see everything else." C.S Lewis – *The Weight of Glory*

Chart Prepared by:
Dr. W.E. Honeycutt - Assistant Professor of Biblical Worldview (Liberty University)

Chapter Three – Biblical Worldview

SALVATION

Affirming a Biblical Worldview

> Romans 5:1-2 (KJV) - *Therefore being justified by faith, we have peace with God through our Lord Jesus Christ: By whom also we have access by faith into this grace wherein we stand, and rejoice in hope of the glory of God.*
>
> Ephesians 2:8-9 (NLT) - *God saved you by his special favor when you believed. And you can't take credit for this; it is a gift from God. Salvation is not a reward for the good things we have done, so none of us can boast about it.*
>
> I Corinthians 6:9,11 (KJV) - *Know ye not that the unrighteous shall not inherit the kingdom of God?... And such were some of you: but ye are washed, but ye are sanctified, but ye are justified in the name of the Lord Jesus, and by the Spirit of our God.*

What does salvation have to do with ethics?

Ethics has to do with how we <u>ought</u> to live. Christian ethics has to do with how a person's faith in Christ and their belief in God's Word should effect how they live in this world. As we understand our salvation, we better appreciate how it enables us to live as we ought.

I. What makes Salvation Necessary?

A. God is absolutely _____ and cannot tolerate the least amount of _____ in His presence. Psalm 5:4, Habakkuk 1:13, 1 John 1:5 (A proper understanding of salvation *begins* with this realization)

> **DEFINITION**
>
> Holy - exalted or worthy of complete devotion as one perfect in goodness and righteousness
>
> http://www.merriam-webster.com/

   a. What is <u>sin</u>? Definition: _____ failure to fulfill or measure up to the law of God either through ignorance, or direct disobedience. Anything less than complete obedience to God's law is sin. James 2:10, 1 John 3:4

B. In my natural state, I am _____, _____ from God and _____ to His wrath. Isaiah 59:1, 2; Romans 1:18, 3:10, 19, 23; 6:23.

C. I am _____ to fulfill God's law. _____ *cannot* please God, remove my sin or deliver me from its consequences or control. Eccl. 7:20, Is. 57:12, 64:6, Ro. 8:5-8, Titus 3:5

D. I am thus _____ and in _____ of eternal separation from God, unless God does something to rescue me. Proverbs 17:15, Romans. 1:18; 6:23, 2 Thessalonians 1:9

Key Biblical Terms Related to Salvation:

1. _____ - Paying the necessary price to purchase another's freedom.
   1 Peter 1:18-19; 1 Cor. 6:19-20

2. _____ or (Born Again) - Giving a second birth to bring about a new life.
   1 Peter 1:3, 17-19; 2 Cor. 5:17

3. _____ – Restoring peace and fellowship to a broken relationship. Col. 1:21-22

4. _____ – Declaring someone free from guilt in a court of law.
   Acts 13:39, Romans 3:24

5. _____ – Setting something apart from common use for exclusive use in the service of God (apart from the world and unto God)   1Cor. 6:11; 1Thess. 4:3-4

6. _____ - Bringing someone else's child into the family to make him/her a genuine family member -   Galatians 4:5-7; Ephesians. 1:4-6; 5:1-8.

7. _____ - Letting someone's offenses go and holding them against them no more. This is remission   Ephesians 1:7; 4:31-32.

SCRIPTURE

Romans 5:1-2 (KJV)
Therefore being justified by faith, we have peace with God through our Lord Jesus Christ:
By whom also we have access by faith into this grace wherein we stand, and rejoice in hope of the glory of God.
Romans 3:23-24 (NLT)
For everyone has sinned; we all fall short of God's glorious standard.
Yet God, with undeserved kindness, declares that we are righteous. He did this through Christ Jesus when he freed us from the penalty for our sins.

Chapter Four - Salvation

II. What makes Salvation Possible?

_____ - "by grace have you been saved"   Ephesians 2:8-9

1. Grace means God acts in kindness to provide something _____.   Titus 3:4-5
2. Grace is demonstrated in the death of Christ on behalf of sinners.   Romans 3:24
3. Grace makes _____ unnecessary in salvation.   Romans 4:4, 11:6; Eph. 2:8-9

Key verses demonstrating the death of Jesus Christ
as the event that makes salvation possible:

-
-
-
-
-

III. What makes Salvation Personal?

A. _____

1. It was central to the teaching of Jesus Christ.
   Mark 1:15; Luke 5:32, 13:3,5, 24:46-47
2. It was central to the teaching of the Apostles.
   a. Peter - Acts 2:38, 3:19, 8:22
   b. Paul - Acts 17:30, 20:21, 26:20

Repentance does not mean:
1. _____ (Judas did that)
2. Simply feeling regret for or sorrow over my sin.
   II Cor, 7:9,10
3. Deciding to become a better person. (Our righteousness means nothing to God. (Isa 64:6)

> "Grace is the good pleasure of God that inclines Him to bestow benefits upon the undeserving. It is a self-existent principle inherent in the divine nature and appears to us as a self-caused propensity to pity the wretched, spare the guilty, welcome the outcast, and bring into favor those who were before under just disapprobation. Its use to us sinful men is to save us and make us sit together in heavenly places to demonstrate to the ages the exceeding riches of God's kindness to us in Christ Jesus."
>
> A.W. Tozer

Chapter Four - Salvation

Repentance means:

1. I realize I am _____ before God who is _____.

    Psalm 51:3,4, Luke 15:18,19, Romans 3:19

2. I have changed my mind about God and sin. The root idea of repentance is "a change of mind."

3. I am willing to experience a visible change in my lifestyle. Luke 3:8, 10-14

B. _____

What faith does and does not mean:

1. Simply believing in God. James 2:19

2. An irrational "blind leap"

    - A mere agreement with the facts of the Gospel.   I Cor. 15:2

    - An purely emotional response to the Gospel.   Mt. 13:5, 20-21

Faith means:

1. I have heard and understood God's provision in Jesus Christ.

    Romans 10:17, I Cor. 15:1-2

2. I have realized that salvation is through Christ alone.

    John 14:6, Acts 4:12, I Tim. 2:5

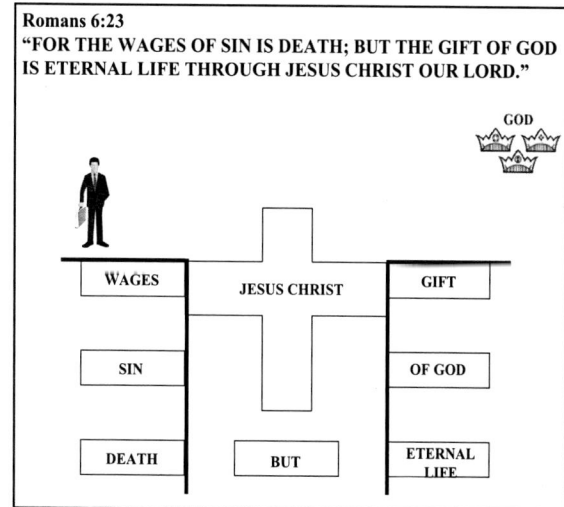 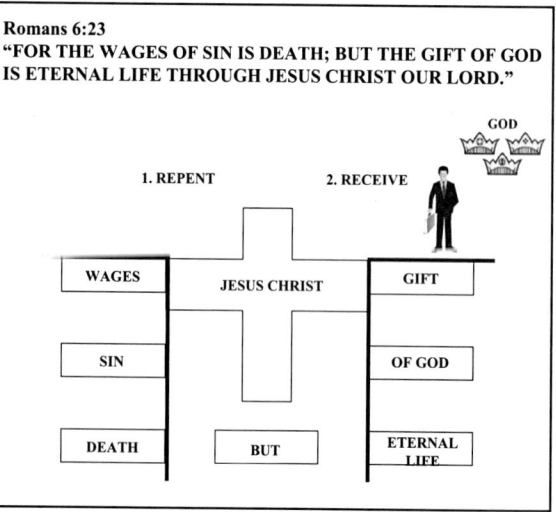

Chapter Four - Salvation

What happens at our conversion?
When we repent and believe, God simultaneously *transfers* our sin record to Christ, and Christ's record of righteousness to us.

1. God imputes **my sin to Christ's account**.
   Isaiah 53:4-6, Romans 3:24-26, 2 Corinthians 5:21, 1 Peter 2:24, 3:18.
2. *God imputes **Christ's righteousness to my account**.*
   Romans 4:5-8, 22-25; 2 Corinthians 5:21

IV. Three Tenses to a Person's Salvation:

A. Past Salvation - _____

1. Defined:

    a. The act of God in which He declares the sinner to be in right standing with himself.

    b. Justification – to "declare righteous or holy"

2. It's place in Salvation:

    a. Past salvation involves permanent deliverance from sin's eternal consequences.

    b. **In Justification God _____ me to live as I ought.**

       Eph.2:10, Titus 3:8 James 2:14-26

B. Present Salvation - _____

1. Defined:

    a. The ongoing work of God in which He develops within the believer a holy lifestyle.

    b. to "set apart"

2. It's place in Salvation:

    a. Present salvation involving progressive deliverance from sin's temporal control.

    b. Sanctification is needed because justification is _____ in its immediate results

Chapter Four - Salvation

c. Sanctification changes my _____ but not my _____.

d. In Sanctification God equips and empowers me to live as I ought.

C. Future Salvation - _____

  1. Defined:

    a. The completion of a believer's salvation when God delivers their body from mortality to immortality and from corruption to incorruption.

    b. I Cor. 15:50-53 Romans 8:23; 13:11

  2. It's place in Salvation:

    a. Future Salvation involving total and complete deliverance from the condition of sin.

    b. This promise of final or completed salvation in glorification inspires me to live as I ought. Romans 13:11-14; 1Peter 1:3-16, 2:11-12; Col. 3:1-10

A Comparison of Justification and Sanctification	
Justification	Sanctification
Justification is free (Jn 4:1).	Sanctification is costly (Lk 14:25-33).
Justification is instantaneous (Jn 3:8).	Sanctification is a life-long process (Jn 8:31).
Justification is by faith (Eph 2:8).	Sanctification is by faithfulness (1 Cor 4:2).
Justification is not of works (Eph 2:9).	Sanctification is of works (Eph 2:10).
Justification involves Christ's love for me (Jn 3:16).	Sanctification involves my love for Christ (1 Jn 4:19).
Justification conce4rns Christ's righteousness (2 Cor 5:21).	Sanctification concerns my righteousness (Lk 14:25-33).
Justification involves my *position* in Christ (Col 2:11-14).	Sanctification involves my *practice* (Col 3:1-11).
Justification considers what God has done (1 Cor 15:3-4).	Sanctification considers what I am doing (Lk 14:25-33).
Justification is God's commitment to me (1 Jn 5:9-13).	Sanctification is my commitment to God (Jn 14:15).
Justification requires obedience to one command: to believe the Gospel (Acts 6:7).	Sanctification requires obedience to all of Christ's commands (Matt 28:19-20).
Justification focuses on the cross which Jesus took up once and for all (1 Cor 1:18).	Sanctification focuses on the cross which I am to take up daily (Lk 9:53).
Justification is finished at the moment of faith (Jn 5:24).	Sanctification is not finished until I go to be with the Lord (1 Cor 9:24-27).

Akin, D. (n.d.). *Grace Community Church*. Retrieved July 2, 2012, from http://storage.cloversites.com/gracecommunitychurch8/documents/Justification%20and%20Sanctification%20chart.pdf

Chapter Five

BIBLICAL ETHICS
Affirming a Biblical Worldview

II Timothy 3:16-17 (NLT)- *All Scripture is inspired by God and is useful to teach us what is true and to make us realize what is wrong in our lives. It straightens us out and teaches us to do what is right. (17) It is God's way of preparing us in every way; fully equipped for every good thing God wants us to do.*

Romans 2:14-15 (NLT) - *Even when Gentiles, who do not have God's written law, instinctively follow what the law says, they show that in their hearts they know right from wrong. (15) They demonstrate that God's law is written within them, for their own consciences either accuse them or tell them they are doing what is right.*

DEFINITION

Ethics deals with what is right and wrong. Christian ethics deals with what is morally right and wrong for a Christian."
Geisler, *Christian Ethics*, (2001, p.17).

- Ethics (plural – noun) moral principles that govern a person's or group's behavior:

Oxford Dictionaries. 2010. Oxford Dictionaries. http://oxforddictionaries.com/definition/ethics (accessed May 30, 2012).

DEFINITION

Schools of ethics in Western philosophy can be divided, very roughly, into three sorts. The *first*, drawing on the work of Aristotle, holds that the virtues (such as justice, charity, and generosity) are dispositions to act in ways that benefit both the person possessing them and that person's society. The *second*, defended particularly by Kant, makes the concept of duty central to morality: humans are bound, from a knowledge of their duty as rational beings, to obey the categorical imperative to respect other rational beings. *Thirdly*, utilitarianism asserts that the guiding principle of conduct should be the greatest happiness or benefit of the greatest number.
Oxford Dictionaries. 2010. Oxford Dictionaries. http://oxforddictionaries.com/definition/ethics (accessed May 30, 2012).

"Ethics as such is interested less in what people in fact do than in what they ought to do, less in what values presently are and more in what their values ought to be."
– *Approaching Moral Decisions*, by Arthur F. Holmes

* The process of how we work through moral issues is called an ethical system.

I. The <u>Origin</u> of the Good and Right – Essentialism

QUESTION – Where does what is right come from?

PLATO – The Euthyphro Dilemma

- Is something right because God wills it or..

- Does God will it because it is right

ANSWER –

II. The Origin of the Good and Right

A. God is _____ nature. Mal. 3:6

B. God's essential nature is perfect _____ and _____. – Isa. 6:3; I John 4:8

C. Whatever _____ _____ flows from His _____. – Ps. 145:17

D. _____ – the root word here is "essence".

In other words good and right flows from the "essence" (dict: fundamental nature) of who God is.

God's Unchanging DNA!
D - _____
N - _____
A - _____

THINKING

Question: Apart from God and a Biblical worldview, what do people base moral truth on?

Question: Can moral truth exist without God?

Question: Are there such things as "moral absolutes"?

III. The <u>Revelation</u> of the Good and Right

QUESTION – How do we come to know the right?

ANSWER –

Chapter Five – Biblical Ethic

How does God reveal Himself and His moral will to man?

    A. _____ - (Psalm 19:1-6)

        In a general way God has revealed, and continues to reveal, His moral will to all mankind.

SCRIPTURE

Romans 2;14-15 (NLT) Even Gentiles, who do not have God's written law, show that they know his law when they instinctively obey it, even without having heard it. (15) They demonstrate that God's law is written in their hearts, for their own conscience and thoughts either accuse them or tell them they are doing right.

We see this evidenced in Man –
(God's creation which has been given moral aptitude)

        1. Our _____ – Rom. 2:14

        2. Our _____ – Rom. 2:15

Conscience (Def.) *That inward faculty, possessed by all of us which, pronounces judgment upon our attitudes and actions as being either right or wrong, and b. prompts us to do right.*

        3. Our _____

        4. Our _____

    B. _____ (Ps. 19:7-11)

God makes known vital truths about Himself which He has not made known in nature.

        QUESTION. *What are examples of "Special Revelation"?*

-
-
-
-

Specifically let us consider His revelation to us though the Scriptures

        1. Its _____

            a. Because of the limits of general revelation.

            b. Because mankind needs a final authority for creed and conduct.

        2. Its _____

            a. It is inspired by God.

Chapter Five – Biblical Ethic

SCRIPTURE

II Timothy 3:16-17 (NLT) All Scripture is inspired by God and is useful to teach us what is true and to make us realize what is wrong in our lives. It corrects us when we are wrong and teaches us to do what is right.
(17) God uses it to prepare and equip his people to do every good work.

John 17:17 (KJV) Sanctify them through thy truth: thy word is truth

    b. Through it God reveals specialized truth about Himself.

3. Its _____

    a. To provide an absolute basis of knowledge concerning the right. – II Tim. 3:16

    b. To change our lives. – II Tim. 3:17; Eph. 5:26,27; John 17:17

4. Its Use

    a. Abuses of Scripture

-
-
-
-

    b. Its Proper Use

       1) _____ - general, non-changing, descriptive truths about God, man, and all creation

       2) _____ - prescriptive truth intended to be a standard or rule which governs human conduct

       3) _____ - rules/standards of conduct which are not specifically addressed in Scripture but are derived from its descriptive and prescriptive truth

IV. General Characteristics of a Biblical Ethic

A. It is based on God's _____.

B. It is dependent upon God's _____.

C. It is authoritative – It is God "breathed" (inspiration)

E. It is prescriptive – It tells us how we should live.

F. It is Absolute -

Chapter Five – Biblical Ethic

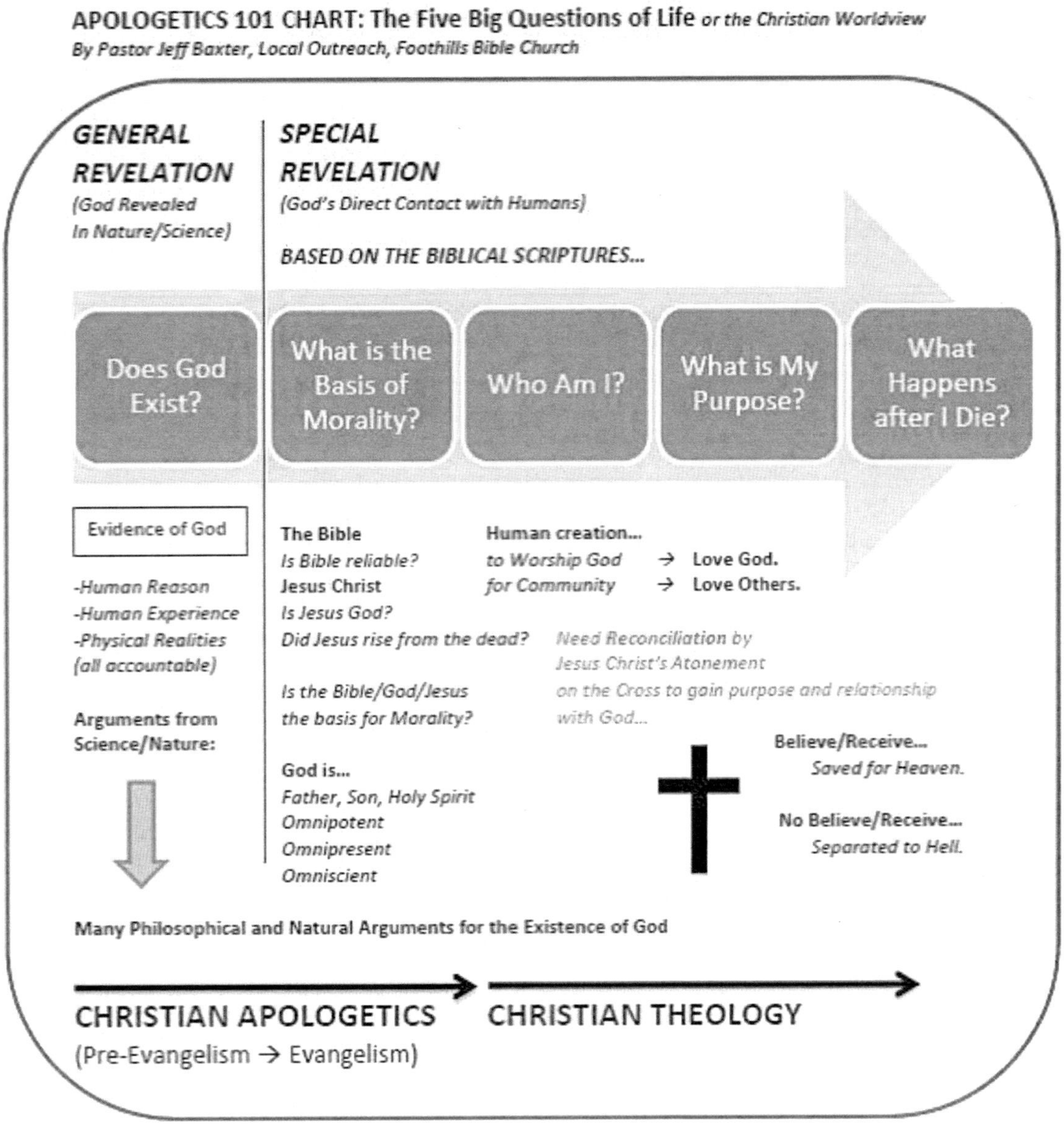

APOLOGETICS 101 CHART: The Five Big Questions of Life or the Christian Worldview
By Pastor Jeff Baxter, Local Outreach, Foothills Bible Church

GENERAL REVELATION (God Revealed In Nature/Science)

SPECIAL REVELATION (God's Direct Contact with Humans)

BASED ON THE BIBLICAL SCRIPTURES…

- Does God Exist?
- What is the Basis of Morality?
- Who Am I?
- What is My Purpose?
- What Happens after I Die?

Evidence of God
- Human Reason
- Human Experience
- Physical Realities (all accountable)

Arguments from Science/Nature:

The Bible
Is Bible reliable?
Jesus Christ
Is Jesus God?
Did Jesus rise from the dead?

Is the Bible/God/Jesus the basis for Morality?

God is…
Father, Son, Holy Spirit
Omnipotent
Omnipresent
Omniscient

Human creation…
to Worship God → Love God.
for Community → Love Others.

Need Reconciliation by Jesus Christ's Atonement on the Cross to gain purpose and relationship with God…

Believe/Receive… Saved for Heaven.

No Believe/Receive… Separated to Hell.

Many Philosophical and Natural Arguments for the Existence of God

CHRISTIAN APOLOGETICS → **CHRISTIAN THEOLOGY**
(Pre-Evangelism → Evangelism)

http://sacredoutfitter.blogspot.com/2012/01/what-does-evangelism-and-apologetics.html

The reliability and trustworthiness of the Bible

1. Confirmation by unity and evidence from the manuscripts

2. Confirmation by Archeology

3. Confirmation by fulfilled Prophecy

4. Confirmation by Scientific and Historical accuracy

Chapter Five – Biblical Ethic

V. Absolutes... Absolutely!

What is an Absolute?

- Free from imperfection or lack: whole entire, the absolute truth.
- With no limits or restrictions: absolute power.
- Absolutely – completely, entirely, without doubt, certainly

A. ABSOLUTISM verses RELATIVISM

What is the difference between a **factual judgement** (e.g., people disapprove of murder) and a **value judgement** (e.g., people ought to disapprove of murder). Are all values **relative,** or are some **absolute** The debate between moral relativism and absolutism is of central importance to ethical reasoning, and this debate is especially pressing in contemporary culture.

(J.P Moreland. *Philosophical Foundations for a Christian Worldview.* Intervarsity Press, 2003)

1. Relative Truth –

Truth that is true at only one time and at one place. It's true to some people and not to others. It's true now but it may not have been true in the past and it may not be again in the future, it's subject to change. It is also subject to perspective of people.

(Note: We will discuss Relativism specifically in the next chapter)

2. Absolute Truth –

Whatever is true at one time and at one place is true at all times and at all places. What is true for one person is true for all persons. Truth is true whether we believe it or not. Truth is discovered or it is revealed, it is not invented by a culture or by religious men.

(Taken from Absolutism verses Relativism http://www.letusreason.org/Apolo1.htm , 2005)

- Norman Geisler - "Since God's moral character does not change, it follows that moral obligations flowing from His nature are absolute"

  (Norman Geisler, *Christian Ethics*, Baker, 2000)

- Jean Paul Sartre – (French Philosopher) Because we see absolutes conflicting there must not be absolutes.

- Joseph Fletcher – "Situational Ethics" The situation determines what we should do therefore there are no moral absolutes

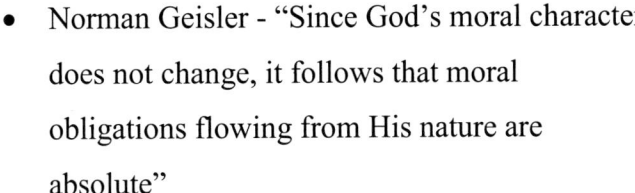

BIOGRAPHY

Sartre – (1905-1980) A French philosopher, novelist, and playwright. He focused his philosophies on the nature of human life and consciousness.

Fletcher (1905–1991) a professor at both Cambridge and Harvard Divinity School, Fletcher expounded the theory of situational ethics in the 1960s. His book is titled, *Situation Ethics: The New Morality*. Fletcher is known for his controversial statements regarding such topics as; abortion, infanticide, euthanasia, eugenics, and cloning.

B. Categories of Moral Crises

Moral Dilemma – A Moral Dilemma is when you must choose one of two things, but either thing would be wrong to do when taking it on its own.

1. Crisis of <u>Knowledge</u> - A seemingly difficult situation which may at first appear to be a moral dilemma, but, in fact, simply requires further information to simplify the decision.

2. Crisis of <u>Conscience</u> - A situation in which you know the right thing to do, but sinful nature tempts you to take the easy way out. It is not a dilemma, it is a question of obedience.

3. Crisis of <u>Absolutes</u> - A true **moral dilemma**. Cases and situations in which the right thing to do is difficult to identify because absolute moral duties at least appear to be in conflict.

C. Three Cases People will use to Question your belief in Absolutism

1. Is it ever right to **LIE?**

   WHAT ABOUT DECEPTION?

   Three types of Deceptions:

   * Not Sin –

   * Clearly Sin –

* Moral Dilemmas -

2. Is it ever right to disobey **AUTHORITIES**?

    * Parents?

    * Government?

    * School/Work ?etc..

3. Is it ever right to take a **KILL SOMEONE?**

    "Thou shalt not kill" – Duet 5:17

    * Capital Punishment?

    * War?

    * Self Defense?

Moral Dilemma – A Moral Dilemma is when you must choose one of two things, but either thing would be wrong to do when taking it on its own.

D. Three Approaches to Absolutes.

(Based on Norman Geisler's Christian Ethics)

1. UNQUALIFIED ABSOLUTISM

(No Exceptions, No Exemptions)

A. The basis for moral absolutes is God's unchanging character.

B. God has expressed his unchanging moral character in his law that is absolute and is not to be broken.

C. God cannot contradict himself.

D. Therefore, no two absolutes can actually conflict. All moral conflicts are only apparent; they are not real.

2. CONFLICTING ABSOLUTISM

(Do the Lesser of two Evils)

A. The basis for moral absolutes is God's unchanging character.

B. God has expressed his unchanging moral character in his law that is absolute and is not to be broken.

C We live in a fallen world; consequently, real moral conflicts do occur.

D. When two duties conflict, you have a moral obligation to both duties.

E. One is to avoid the greater sin, confess the lesser sin, and ask for forgiveness.

3. GRADED ABSOLUTISM

(Do the Greater Good) — Not the greater results but the higher rule.

A. The basis for moral absolutes is God's unchanging character.

B. God has expressed his unchanging moral character in his law that is absolute and is not to be broken.

C. We live in a fallen world; consequently, real moral conflicts do occur.

D. There are higher and lower laws. There are no <u>exceptions</u> to absolute moral laws only <u>exemptions</u> from obeying them in view of higher ones.

E. One is to do the greater good and guilt is not imputed.

	UNQUALIFIED ABSOLUTISM	CONFLICTING ABSOLUTISM	GRADED ABSOLUTISM
Distinguishing emphasis	No exemptions No exceptions	Do the "lesser" evil.	Do the "greater" good (higher moral law)
Lie to save a life?	NO	YES	YES
Is it sin?	--	YES	NO
Seek forgiveness?	--	YES	NO

RAHAB – Class Discussion

Read: Exodus 20:13, 16; Joshua 2:1-7; Hebrews 11:31; James 2:25; Titus 1:2
1. What does the Bible say about telling the truth and lying?
2. Did God hold Rahab accountable for her lie?
3. Why do you think that God rewards Rahab? (Hebrews & James)

Chapter Six

CHRISTIAN LIBERTIES

Affirming a Biblical Worldview

Romans 14:1-5 (NIV) *(1) Accept him whose faith is weak, without passing judgment on disputable matters. (2) One man's faith allows him to eat everything, but another man, whose faith is weak, eats only vegetables. (3) The man who eats everything must not look down on him who does not, and the man who does not eat everything must not condemn the man who does, for God has accepted him. (4) Who are you to judge someone else's servant? To his own master he stands or falls. And he will stand, for the Lord is able to make him stand. (5) One man considers one day more sacred than another; another man considers every day alike. Each one should be fully convinced in his own mind.*

I Corinthians 8:9 (NIV) *Be careful, however, that the exercise of your freedom does not become a stumbling block to the weak.*

I Corinthians 6:12 (NIV) *Everything is permissible for me--but not everything is beneficial. Everything is permissible for me--but I will not be mastered by anything.*

I. Essential Definitions

A. **Ethical gray area:**

An area that is not specifically addressed in Scripture and is therefore viewed as permissible by some Christians.

Examples:

B. **Stronger brother:**

One who participates in an ethical gray area in full assurance of his conscience because of his understanding of Christian freedom.

Note: This does not necessarily mean he is more mature in the faith than a weaker brother.

C. Weaker brother:

One who does not participate in an ethical gray area because of the sensitivity of his conscience: his participation would be a sin to him

Note: This does not necessarily mean he is less mature in the faith than a stronger brother.

D. Stumbling block:

An action taken by a stronger brother which, though it would ordinarily qualify as a permissible act of freedom, influences a weaker brother to sin against his conscience.

One of these key passages dealing with this subject is Romans chapters 14-15 where Paul addresses the situation by dividing the participants into two distinct camps. One he calls the "weak" (14:2) and the other "strong" (15:1). The strong he describes as those individuals with more freedom of conscience and the weak as those whose freedom is limited by more restrictions. Paul is not making a statement of strong versus weak in relation to which is more spiritual, rather the distinction is in made in regards to the ability to keep one's conscience pure. In fact, Paul gives admonitions and warnings to both (see chart below)

The Weaker Brother (Romans 14)	The Stronger Brother (Romans 14, 15:1)
Both are believers and brothers/sisters in Christ (v. 1, 8, 10)	
Both are seeking to thank and honor God in the actions (v.6, 8)	
Does not eat meat only vegetables (v.2)	Eats both meat and vegetables (v.2)
Observes certain days as holy/sacred (v.5)	Sees all days as the same (v.5)
Does not drink wine (v.21)	Drinks wine (v.21)

The Weaker Brother (Romans 14) Improper response	The Stronger Brother (Romans 14, 15:1) Improper response
Judges or condemns the stronger brother (v.3, 10)	Looks down on the weaker brother (v.3, 10)

The Weaker Brother (Romans 14) Paul's admonitions	The Stronger Brother (Romans 14, 15:1) Paul's admonitions
Do not judge your brother (v.3, 13)	Do not look down upon your brother (v.3, 10)
Do not do it if you believe it to be wrong (Listen to your conscience) (v.2, 5, 14)	
Do not cause your brother to stumble or fall into sin (vss.13-15)	
Both will give account to God (v.4, 10-12)	

II. Principles

A. _____.

    1. We must be true to ourselves and not act simply on the opinions of others.

    2. Rom 14:5

    3. Rom 14:22-23

B. _____.

    1. If we are confident that what we are engaged in will pass our Lord's scrutiny at the judgment day, we should continue; if not, we should refrain.

    2. Rom 14:6-12

C. _____.

    1. Rom 14:6-12

    2. To "offend" here does not mean to make angry, but rather to cause another believer to act in such a way

    3. "Am I my brothers keeper?" – Cain! The spiritual truth is that we are our brothers keeper! (Rom 14:15-20, 15:1-6)

    4. Liberty is great! _____ is better. (Eph 4:3, 11-16)

    5. We are here to _____ one another, not tear down.

D. _____.

    1. I Cor 10:27-33

    2. Paul was burdened enough about the unsaved that he restricted himself in doing only what enhanced the gospel in their eyes.

> **SCRIPTURE**
>
> **I Timothy 1:18-19** (NLT)
> Timothy, my son, here are my instructions for you, based on the prophetic words spoken about you earlier. May they help you fight well in the Lord's battles.
> Cling to your faith in Christ, and keep your conscience clear. For some people have deliberately violated their consciences; as a result, their faith has been shipwrecked.

> **SCRIPTURE**
>
> **Ephesians 4:1-4** (NLT)
> I, therefore, the prisoner of the Lord, beseech you to walk worthy of the calling with which you were called, with all lowliness and gentleness, with longsuffering, bearing with one another in love,
> endeavoring to keep the unity of the Spirit in the bond of peace.
> [There is] one body and one Spirit, just as you were called in one hope of your calling;

Chapter Six – Christian Liberty

III. Guidelines

A. **Principles of** _____

   Will it be spiritually profitable? I Cor. 6:12

B. **Principle of** _____

   Will it build me up? I Cor. 10:23

C. **Principle of** _____

   Will it slow me down in the race? Heb 12:1

D. **Principle of** _____

   Will it bring me into bondage? I Cor. 6:12

E. **Principle of** _____

   Will it hypocritically cover my sin? I Peter 2:16

F. **Principle of** _____

   Will it violate the Lordship of Christ in my life? Rom. 14:1-8

G. **Principle of** _____

   Will it help other Christians by its example?   I Cor. 8:9

H. **Principle of** _____

   Will it lead others to Christ? I Cor. 10:27-29

I. **Principle of** _____

   Would Jesus do it? I John 2:6

J. **Principle of** _____

   Will it glorify God? I Cor. 10:31

(Adapted from a sermon by Dr. John MacArthur Jnr.)

Chapter Six – Christian Liberty

A Summary on Christian Liberty

L - _____
I - _____
B - _____
E - _____
R - _____
T - _____
Y - _____

"Perhaps we should see LIBERTY as a gift that is only <u>gained</u> when it is <u>given</u>, not a <u>right</u> as much as a <u>responsibility</u>, and is best exemplified in <u>peace</u> not <u>pride</u>!"

Chapter Six – Christian Liberty

Chapter Seven

HINDUSIM as a Worldview
Affirming a Biblical Worldview

I Peter 3:15 (KJV) - *But sanctify the Lord God in your hearts: and [be] ready always to [give] an answer to every man that asketh you a reason of the hope that is in you with meekness and fear:*

John 14:6 (KJV) - *Jesus saith unto him, I am the way, the truth, and the life: no man cometh unto the Father, but by me.*

John 17:14-17 (NIV) - *I have given them your word and the world has hated them, for they are not of the world any more than I am of the world. (15) My prayer is not that you take them out of the world but that you protect them from the evil one. (16) They are not of the world, even as I am not of it. (17) Sanctify them by the truth; your word is truth.*

I. Name, Key Symbol and Number of Followers

A. **Dharma** – righteousness, duty; "Hinduism" a later word applied to people of Indus Valley, now accepted by natives.
B. Meaning of symbol "*OM*"
C. The third largest world religion; roughly 900 m. Hindus worldwide (14% of all religious adherents). About 1 m. in U. S.

II. Brief History

A. **The Vedic Period** (1500 to 300 B.C. – no one really knows)
B. **The Upanishads** (800-400 B.C.)
C. **Modern Hinduism** - Unlike Buddhism, Christianity and Islam, Hinduism has no single founder, and it is also impossible to say exactly what Hinduism is in terms of religious beliefs because there is no one way of understanding "god."

III. Sacred Writings

A. The Vedas
   1. Largely polytheistic; worship of many gods (symbolizing natural forces).

2. Brahmanism (leadership by priests) predominant – custodians of elaborate and tedious sacrificial system to thank and appease gods. (*Brahmanas* – priestly manuals*)*

3. Philosophy of *Upanishads*, also called *Vedanta* ("end" of the Vedas) more prominent in Hinduism today. Only Hindu scholars learn and study *Vedas* now.

B. The Upanishads

1. Philosophical basis of Hinduism today.
2. Essentially philosophical commentaries on the rest of the Vedic writings.
3. Teach *advaita, or* "non-dualist" view of the universe (no spirit and matter, just all spirit (*Brahman*)
4. More characteristically monistic (non-dualistic/pantheistic), conveying the idea that all
    a. Reality is in essence *One*—*Brahman*, which manifests itself in the many
    b. powers or gods, and is the true essence of all things. Polytheism.
5. Central idea - "*Atman* is *Brahman*" summed up in "**tat tvam asi**," lit. "*You are That.*"

C. The Epics

1. Mahabharata *(Between 540 and 300 B.C. "The great Bharata" – a family name)*

2. Bhagavad-*Gita (Bet. 1000-900 B.C.; Lit. "Song of the Supreme Lord;" Abbreviate "Gita*") - 18 chapters of Book 6 of *Mahabharata* Featuring Lord Krishna (eighth *avatar* of Vishnu), a very popular deity in modern Hindusim.

3. Main subjects of the *Gita,*
    a. Way of salvation explained from philosophy of *Upanishads*.
    b. Indestructibility of the *Atman and its* oneness with *Brahman*
    c. Duties (*dharma*) of caste
    d. Karma, samsara* and *moksha,*
    e. Supreme value of *yoga (*especially *karma* and *bhakti)*
    f. Krishna reveals self as Supreme being over all gods and people (Gita 4.06, 10).

DEFINITION

Avatar –
1. Hindu Mythology . the descent of a deity to the earth in an incarnate form or some manifest shape; the incarnation of a god.
2. an embodiment or personification, as of a principle, attitude, or view of life.
3. Digital Technology . a graphical image that represents a person, as on the Internet.

www.dictionary.com

IV. Core Beliefs of Hindu Scriptures

Important: This is not a creed or "doctrinal statement" for determining whether someone is or is not a Hindu. They are not required beliefs, but presently beliefs held by most Hindus.

1. **Brahman** – Most Hindus believe that ultimate Reality is *Brahman*

2. **Atman** – all humans possess an *atman*, or eternal and indestructible soul/self and its ultimate destiny and purpose is to be united to *Brahman* the true Self.
   Note: Realizing that *atman is Brahman* is to achieve the highest or perfect knowledge, according to Hinduism.

3. **Maya** – Our perceptions are actually *maya*, which means "illusion" or "appearance;" that is, what we experience in our existence, in the natural worlds, is not the really real, kind of like a dream or a mirage—it appears real and we may act as though it is real, but it is an illusion, it is an "illusive power" (*Gita* 3.29)

4. **Samsara** – We are caught up in the illusory world of *maya* because of our desires and attachments to the world and its pleasures. As long as the *atman* does not realize that it is really *Brahman*, it remains locked in the potentially endless earthly cycle of birth, death and rebirth called *samsara*, or literally "a wandering across."

Samsara; **The endless cycles of death and rebirth**

 **THINKING**

Question: Is the biblical concept of "reaping what you sow" (Job 4:8), the same as Karma?

"Many religions and philosophies promote the concept of karma: If you do something good, good will return to you, and if you do something bad, you'll experience something bad as a result. But if you really reap what you sow, then every mistake you make will keep haunting you. Jesus offers a much better way to live - with grace"

http://www.crosswalk.com/faith/spiritual-life/reaping-what-you-sow-christian-karma-11637464.html
Mark Herringshaw, <u>The Karma of Jesus: Do We Really Reap What We Sow?</u>, Bethany House, 2009

5. **Karma** – The law of *karma* (cause and effect based on actions/deeds)

* Keeps people locked in *samsara* (even "good" karma).
* Depending on *karma*, may be reincarnated (or return in another physical body) as a human, an animal or even a plant.
* Good karma still a curse, but has some benefits Temporary heavenly time, then reincarnation in higher caste (thus one step closer to *moksha*)

Chapter Seven – Hinduism (Religious Worldview)

6. **Moksha/Nirvana** – The hope in Hinduism, the salvation for which Hindus strive, is *moksha*. This is "liberation" from *samsara*.

7. **Caste** - This was a hierarchy of social privilege and responsibility based on one's *karma* from a past life. (*Gita* 18.41-44).

   - Closely associated with *dharma* - Social "duty" and moral obligations that fall to people due to their caste.
   - Karma determines *caste* and *caste* determines *dharma*.
   - Divinely established system (*Gita* 18.41-44 also *Laws of Manu*—the first man; have detailed explanations of caste). Four original castes, with a fifth added. Hundreds of sub castes in India today. Castes are not to socialize or intermarry.
     - *Brahmin* – religious leaders/teachers and nobility
     - K*shatriya* – military and administrators of society
     - *Vaishyas* – manual laborers, like craftsmen, farmers and merchants
     - *Shudras* - duty (*dharma*) it was to serve the higher castes
     - *Dalit* – In time, Hindus also identified another caste, the *dalit* or "untouchables," who were the lowest of the low in terms of poverty and lack of privilege.

God or Gods?

Brahman - While Hindus believe in *Brahman* and define this as the Supreme and Absolute Reality; the Eternal, the Infinite and the Indivisible Existence, the Self, they also believe that *Brahman* manifests itself in "various powers" these being the many gods and goddesses of Hinduism. Hindus may, therefore, claim that there is only one god, *Brahman*, or any number of the hundreds of millions of lesser deities that they devote themselves to in hopes to achieve *moksha*. This is why Hindus can say there is one god and many gods at the same time.

In modern Hinduism there are three main deities the *Trimurti or* "triad" (but essentially 300 m. deities and sub deities as well!).
- Brahma (the Creator),
- Vishnu (the Preserver),
- Siva (the Destroyer)

V. Summarizing Hinduism's plan of salvation:

1. *What is salvation?* – *Moksha* – liberation from *samsara* Main idea—performing daily duties (dharma) and disciplines in view of union (yoking) with *Brahman*.

2. *What makes salvation necessary?* – *Karma* and *samsara* – We are locked into this never-ending cycle because we have not renounced earthly pleasures and sought union with Brahman. We are ignorant of this true knowledge which keeps us trapped in the illusion.

3. *What makes salvation possible?* – The explanations found in the Hindu Scriptures, especially the *Gita* where Krishna tells his followers how to be united to Brahman; the Supreme.

4. *What makes salvation personal?* – Renunciation of earthly pleasures, fulfilling *dharma (caste duty)*, practicing *yoga* (focusing mind and body on achieving union with Brahman)

VI. Some Biblical Perspective on Hinduism

 **SCRIPTURE**

Genesis 1:1 (KJV)
In the beginning God created the heaven and the earth.

Genesis 1:27 (KJV)
So God created man in his [own] image, in the image of God created he him; male and female created he them.

Some claim that Hinduism is the "oldest" of the world religions, suggesting it's the beginning of man's religious thought. Christians would have to disagree with this. In Genesis we see the oldest human "religion" and civilization. Biblical narrative conveys that there is one God who created humans in His image and likeness as one male and one female initially; these first humans then fell into corruption. They acquired a sin nature which somehow affected their heart which became "evil only continually." But God promised redemption to these humans and covered their original sins with animal skins, instituting the need for sacrificial atonement to pay for sin. When humanity became utterly corrupt, God destroyed the world through a worldwide, catastrophic flood, after which Noah's family became the basis of all current civilizations, including that which settled in the Indus Valley. In Genesis Chapter 10 we see how from Noah and his sons descended all the nations (10:32). In chapter 11 we learn how the world was populated from the incident at Babel. Languages changed and people dispersed.

Once these early ancestors spread out, they took ideas of the true religion—the true story of humankind regarding *creation, the fall, the need for sacrificial atonement for sins*, and *the flood* to many other parts of the world, they eventually, due to their sin nature, distorted these ideas into polytheism - assigning separate gods to the parts of creation (which early Hinduism did)—but still retained ideas consistent with a biblical theology; like an *original creation*, a *worldwide flood, moral obligations*, etc. Paul, in fact, states clearly that *humanity has always known the truth about God, but, due to their sinfulness, suppressed that truth*, and "exchanged the truth of God for a lie, and worshipped and served the creature more than the Creator (Romans 1:19-25)." The multiple depictions of Hindus gods as animals, humans and mixtures of both, is part of the distortion when they "changed the glory of the incorruptible God into images of corruptible man, and birds and four-footed beasts and creeping things (Romans 1:23).

We should not be surprised that we find similarities in religions like Hinduism, because God created the human heart (Psalm 33:15) and placed eternity (Ecclesiastes 3:11) and a sense of morality (Romans 2:14-15) in it. Religions, thus, always convey morality (and very similar ones at that) and a sense of eternal life no matter where they are in the world; what we might call a sense of always (a yearning for immortality) and a sense of ought (an inescapable sense of moral law).

SCRIPTURE

Romans 2:14-15 (KJV)
For when the Gentiles, which have not the law, do by nature the things contained in the law, these, having not the law, are a law unto themselves
Which shew the work of the law written in their hearts, their conscience also bearing witness, and [their] thoughts the mean while accusing or else excusing one another;)

John 3:16-19 (KJV)
For God so loved the world, that he gave his only begotten Son, that whosoever believeth in him should not perish, but have everlasting life. For God sent not his Son into the world to condemn the world; but that the world through him might be saved.
He that believeth on him is not condemned: but he that believeth not is condemned already, because he hath not believed in the name of the only begotten Son of God.
And this is the condemnation, that light is come into the world, and men loved darkness rather than light, because their deeds were evil.

SALVATION COMPARISON CHART

	Islam	Buddhism	Hinduism	Christianity
WHAT IS SALVATION?	Being **rewarded** on Judgment Day with entrance into Paradise if one's righteous deeds are determined to outweigh their sinful deeds	Achievement of *Nirvana* – "**Cessation**" of desire and the suffering that comes from desire, including the cycles of death and rebirth.	Achievement of *Moksha* - "**Liberation**" from the painful cycle of death and rebirth. **Realization** of one's unity with Ultimate Reality (*Brahman*)	Being **rescued** from sin's eternal consequences, temporal control and actual condition. **Receiving** eternal life as a **gift of grace**
WHAT MAKES SALVATION NECESSARY?	Humans are ignorant of their true nature as a Muslim (submitter) and destined for Hell's fire until they submit to Allah's will	Humans are **enslaved** by *karma* to *samsara* **because of their desire** for the impermanent things of this world, and experience endless **suffering** due to this.	Humans, because of *karma*, are trapped in the cycle of death and rebirth (*samsara*) because of their **ignorance** of Ultimate Reality, and attachment to worldly illusion (*maya*)	Humans are **sinful**, and are **separated** from and **subject to the eternal wrath** of a Holy and Righteous God
WHAT MAKES SALVATION POSSIBLE?	The ***Qur'an*** which teaches humans of their true identity as Muslims who must willingly submit to the will of Allah..	The **enlightenment, example and teachings** of Siddhartha Gautama who became the Buddha through overcoming his desire.	The **knowledge** found in the Hindu Scriptures about escaping *karma* and *samsara* and achieving *moksha* and one's ultimate unity with *Brahman*.	***Divine initiative:*** God through **love** and **grace** reveals the **gospel** and provides to rescue humans from sin through the substitutionary **death and resurrection of Jesus Christ**.
WHAT MAKES SALVATION PERSONAL?	**Human Effort:** Confessing the *Shahada*; believing the **Articles of Faith** and practicing the **Five Pillars of Islam**.	**Human Effort:** Accepting the **Four Noble Truths** and following the **Noble Eightfold Path**. Taking refuge in the Buddha, *Dhamma* (his teachings) and *Sangha* (community of fellow Buddhists).	**Human effort:** Becoming a **yogi** (one who practices yoga, a discipline by which can realize oneness with Ultimate Reality); **Living faithfully** to one's given station in life (*caste* and *dharma*).	**Repentance and faith;** Owning up to and turning from one's sin and turning to the Savior, Jesus Christ, alone for salvation and submitting to him as the Lord.
WHAT IS THE RELATIONSHIP BETWEEN SALVATION AND MORALITY?	Salvation (earning Paradise) possible only **through** faithfully **living a moral life** as defined by *Qur'an* and *Sunnah* to be determined on Judgment Day.	**Salvation is the result of** rigorously living **a moral life** as articulated in the Noble Eightfold Path and the Five precepts (Ten precepts if a monk or nun).	Salvation (*moksha*) **is the result of a moral life**, but especially being a yogi and following the discipline of yoga to focus in union with Brahman.	The **moral life is the result of salvation**. When one receives Christ they are empowered through the Holy spirit to live as they ought and to please God by following Jesus' moral example.

Chapter Seven – Hinduism (Religious Worldview)

Chapter Eight

BUDDHISM as a Worldview
Affirming a Biblical Worldview

I Peter 3:15 (KJV) - *But sanctify the Lord God in your hearts: and [be] ready always to [give] an answer to every man that asketh you a reason of the hope that is in you with meekness and fear:*

John 14:6 (KJV) - *Jesus saith unto him, I am the way, the truth, and the life: no man cometh unto the Father, but by me.*

John 17:14-17 (NIV) - *I have given them your word and the world has hated them, for they are not of the world any more than I am of the world. (15) My prayer is not that you take them out of the world but that you protect them from the evil one. (16) They are not of the world, even as I am not of it. (17) Sanctify them by the truth; your word is truth.*

I. Name, Key Symbol and Number of Followers

A. *Buddha* and *Buddhism* -

B. The Wheel of Dharma (or Dhamma), or Dharma/Dhamma Wheel, -

C. Fourth largest world religion, about 400 m. Buddhists worldwide (about 6% of all religious believers) and 1.5 m. Buddhists in the U.S.

> *"The best of all paths is the Eightfold Path. The best of all truths are the Four Noble Truths. Non-attachment is the best of all states. The best of all men is the Seeing One (the Buddha). This is the only Way. There is none other for the purity of vision. Everything else is . . . deceit"*
> The Buddha, *Dhamappada* 20:273-274

II. Brief History

A. A Renegade Hindu

1. A royal birthright Buddhism was founded by Siddhartha Gautama during the sixth century B.C. His life (563-483 B.C.) coincides with the time when the people of Judah were exiled in Babylon.

Chapter Eight – Buddhism (Religious Worldview)

2. Four Signs

   3. The Great Renunciation

   B. Discovering the Middle Path

   1. Life offers only *dukkha*, -

   2. Six years of asceticism -

   3. The Middle Path/*Dhamma* -

III. Central Principles and Practices of Buddhism

The Four Noble Truths

1. **The First Noble Truth (The certainty of suffering):** Life consists of suffering (dukkha). This concept of suffering includes the experiences of pain, misery, sorrow, and unfulfillment.
2. **The Second Noble Truth (The source/cause of suffering):** Everything is impermanent and ever-changing (the doctrine of *anicca*). We suffer because we desire those things that are impermanent.
3. **The Third Noble Truth (The cessation/cure of suffering):** The way to liberate oneself from suffering is by eliminating all desire. We must stop craving that which is temporary.
4. **The Fourth Noble Truth (The path to the cessation of suffering):** Desire can be eliminated by following the Eightfold Path, which consists of eight points that can be categorized according to three major sections:

The Practice of Buddhism (The Noble Eightfold Path)

Wisdom (*Panna*)
   1. Right Understanding
   2. Right Thought
Ethical Conduct (*Sila*)
   3. Right Speech
   4. Right Action

5. Right Livelihood

Mental Discipline (*Smadhi*)

6. Right Effort

7. Right Awareness

8. Right Meditation

Further Principles of Buddhism

> **THINKING**
> These eight points are not steps to be taken in sequential order, but are attitudes and actions to be developed simultaneously
> The first two points, moreover, serve as the foundation from which the other points flow.

Nirvana *in Buddhism (The Goal)*
- Not heaven or paradise, not a place that one goes when they die
- A passionless state where one feels neither love nor hate
- Literal meaning of Nirvana

IV. Sacred Writings

1. *Tipitaka* - The "Three Baskets"
2. *Sutta-Pitaka* -
   - The *Dhamapadda** -
   - The *Jatakas* -
3. *Vinaya Pitaka* –
4. *Abhidhamma Pitaka* -

V. Becoming a Buddhist

It has become quite common in Buddhism to speak of the Three Jewels or Refuges of:

1. The *Buddha* – What he experienced and the example he left behind
2. The *Dhamma* - What the Buddha taught; The "Way of Truth"
3. The *Sangha* – The community of followers Buddha established who have chosen to follow the Buddha's example and teachings.

Note: Becoming a Buddhist does not require any official ceremony; but often when a would-be follower recited the phrase; " I go for refuge in the Buddha, I go for refuge in the Dhamma and I go for refuge in the Sangha."

VI. Summarizing Buddhism's Plan of Salvation

A. *What is salvation?* – Liberation from suffering and what causes it, achieving Nirvana

B. *What makes salvation necessary?* – Potentially endless cycles of rebirth and death (samsara)

C. *What makes salvation possible?* – the Buddha's personal discovery, example and teachings

D. *What makes salvation personal?* – Believing the Four Noble Truths and practicing the Noble Eightfold Path.

Some Biblical Perspective on Buddhism

 **THINKING**

"The essential teachings and ministries of Jesus and Buddha cannot be reconciled or synthesized. No amount of religious tolerance or pluralism can erase the deep and sharp differences between these two identities, their worldviews, and their actions. By accurately defining these differences we do justice to both religious leaders while communicating the truth in love to those who would place them on the same plane."

Douglas R Groothuis, http://www.equip.org/articles/jesus-and-buddha/ July 2012

Some suggest that Jesus and Buddha really taught essentially the same things, that their doctrines are compatible. This is both true in not true in this way. From an ethical perspective, Buddhism has a lot of merit in that Gautama's and Jesus' moral doctrines are similar. This, we could attribute to the moral law of God "written on the heart" (Romans 2:14-15) and should not find it surprising that all religions, not just Buddhism, teach very similar moral principles. Because of this, much of the ethical teaching and stories of Gautama can be illuminating and illustrative to Jesus' followers.

But here is where the comparison ends. Theologically, Jesus and Gautama are at two opposite poles. Jesus was a monotheist and believed in and taught that God was personal and could be related to as intimately as a "Father" who created man and woman in his image and sustains His creation in a very active way. Jesus taught and modeled prayer to the Father. His use of the intimate term "Abba" is quite significant in this regard. (Mk 14:36) He teaches his followers to pray "Our Father Who is in Heaven (Matthew 6:9) this intimacy with God as a personal, heavenly Father is also taught by Paul (Romans 8:15, Galatians 4:6).

Jesus also believed the source of our sorrows came from within, due to an indwelling sin nature and core corruption, not merely desire or craving (Mark 7:21-22). So a huge and significant contrast is that Jesus taught that we needed to be forgiven of sin by our Heavenly Father

(Matthew 6:12). He also taught about the Kingdom of Heaven as though it were a place in the afterlife that one could aspire to and dwell in, as well as a present reality (Matthew 5:20), and thus escape the condemnation of a literal hell, about which He taught and warned even more than He did heaven. Jesus also spoke of death and resurrection and a final judgment (John 5:29), never reincarnation.

Probably of the greatest significance is the contrast in how Jesus and Gautama thought of themselves and their importance for humanity. Gautama told his followers not to remember him, *per se,* but his teachings as the most important thing. In fact, contrary to popular opinion, Gautama was quite adamant that his teachings were superior to all others. He taught, "The best of ways is the eightfold; the best of truths the four words (noble truths); the best of virtues passionlessness,. *This is the way, there is no other* that leads to the purifying of intelligence. Go on this way! Everything else is . . . deceit. (*Dhamapadda* 20:273-4). Jesus, on the other hand did not point to his teachings as "the way" but rather to Himself as *the* way, *the* truth and *the* life." (John 14:6) His disciples/apostles followed suit when they pronounced "neither is there salvation in any other, for there is no other name under heaven given among men by which we must be saved" (Acts 4:12)

SCRIPTURE

John 14:6 (KJV)
Jesus saith unto him, I am the way, the truth, and the life: no man cometh unto the Father, but by me.

Acts 4:12 (KJV)
Neither is there salvation in any other: for there is none other name under heaven given among men, whereby we must be saved.

John 3:16-19 (KJV)
For God so loved the world, that he gave his only begotten Son, that whosoever believeth in him should not perish, but have everlasting life. For God sent not his Son into the world to condemn the world; but that the world through him might be saved.
He that believeth on him is not condemned: but he that believeth not is condemned already, because he hath not believed in the name of the only begotten Son of God.
And this is the condemnation, that light is come into the world, and men loved darkness rather than light, because their deeds were evil.

This cannot be overemphasized. While Jesus was humble and considered one wise who built his life on His teachings (Matthew 7:24-27), He unequivocally conveyed that getting his identity right was critical to our eternal well-being. "Who do you say that I am?" (Matthew 16:15), "If you do not believe that I am He, you will die in your sins." (John 8:24) "He who does not believe the Son does not have life . . . but God's wrath abides on him." (John 3:18) and "No one comes to the Father except through me." (John 14:6). Jesus made it clear that remembering Him (Luke 22:19) and believing in Him alone for salvation was critical to being His follower and entering the kingdom of Heaven to live eternally with God; there was no other way. So while Gautama taught high moral principles, and claimed to point the way, leaving us some great quotes and illustrations, Jesus Christ was far more than a great moral teacher, and claimed to *be* the way.

SALVATION COMPARISON CHART

	Islam	Buddhism	Hinduism	Christianity
WHAT IS SALVATION?	Being **rewarded** on Judgment Day with entrance into Paradise if one's righteous deeds are determined to outweigh their sinful deeds	Achievement of *Nirvana* – "Cessation" of desire and the suffering that comes from desire, including the cycles of death and rebirth.	Achievement of *Moksha* - "Liberation" from the painful cycle of death and rebirth. **Realization** of one's unity with Ultimate Reality (*Brahman*)	Being **rescued** from sin's eternal consequences, temporal control and actual condition. **Receiving eternal life as a gift of grace**
WHAT MAKES SALVATION NECESSARY?	Humans are ignorant of their true nature as a Muslim (submitter) and destined for Hell's fire until they submit to Allah's will	Humans are **enslaved** by *karma* to *samsara* **because of** their desire for the impermanent things of this world, and experience endless **suffering** due to this.	Humans, because of *karma*, are trapped in the cycle of death and rebirth (*samsara*) because of their **ignorance** of Ultimate Reality, and attachment to worldly illusion (*maya*)	Humans are **sinful**, and are **separated** from and **subject to the eternal wrath** of a Holy and Righteous God
WHAT MAKES SALVATION POSSIBLE?	The *Qur'an* which teaches humans of their true identity as Muslims who must willingly submit to the will of Allah.	The enlightenment, example and teachings of Siddhartha Gautama who became the Buddha through overcoming his desire.	The **knowledge** found in the Hindu Scriptures about escaping *karma* and *samsara* and achieving *moksha* and one's ultimate unity with *Brahman*.	*Divine initiative:* God through **love** and **grace** reveals the **gospel** and provides to rescue humans from sin through the substitutionary **death and resurrection of Jesus Christ**.
WHAT MAKES SALVATION PERSONAL?	*Human Effort:* **Confessing** the *Shahada*; believing the **Articles of Faith** and practicing the **Five Pillars of Islam**.	*Human Effort:* Accepting the **Four Noble Truths** and following the **Noble Eightfold Path**. Taking refuge in the Buddha, *Dhamma* (his teachings) and *Sangha* (community of fellow Buddhists).	*Human effort:* Becoming a **yogi** (one who practices yoga, a discipline by which can realize oneness with Ultimate Reality); **Living** faithfully to one's given station in life (*caste* and *dharma*).	**Repentance and faith;** Owning up to and turning from one's sin and turning to the Savior, Jesus Christ, alone for salvation and submitting to him as the Lord.
WHAT IS THE RELATIONSHIP BETWEEN SALVATION AND MORALITY?	**Salvation** (earning Paradise) possible only **through** faithfully **living a moral life** as defined by *Qur'an* and *Sunnah* to be determined on Judgment Day.	**Salvation is the result of** rigorously living **a moral life** as articulated in the Noble Eightfold Path and the Five precepts (Ten precepts if a monk or nun).	Salvation (*moksha*) **is the result of a moral life**, but especially being a yogi and following the discipline of yoga to focus in union with Brahman.	The **moral life is the result of salvation**. When one receives Christ they are empowered through the Holy spirit to live as they ought to and to please God by following Jesus' moral example.

Chapter Nine

ISLAM as a Worldview
Affirming a Biblical Worldview

I Peter 3:15 (KJV) - But sanctify the Lord God in your hearts: and [be] ready always to [give] an answer to every man that asketh you a reason of the hope that is in you with meekness and fear:

John 14:6 (KJV) - Jesus saith unto him, I am the way, the truth, and the life: no man cometh unto the Father, but by me.

John 17:14-17 (NIV) - I have given them your word and the world has hated them, for they are not of the world any more than I am of the world. (15) My prayer is not that you take them out of the world but that you protect them from the evil one. (16) They are not of the world, even as I am not of it. (17) Sanctify them by the truth; your word is truth.

I. Name, Key Symbol and Number of Followers

A. *Islam, Muslim* - The word Islam means "submission" and refers to the lifestyle of the true "Muslim" (submitter) in submission to the one God's will.

B. The crescent moon and star – (Origin unknown but generally associated with Islam)

C. Second largest world religion, about 1.5 b. Muslims worldwide (nearly 21% of all religious believers). About 1.6 m. Muslims in the U.S.

II. Brief History

A. An Orphan in Mecca

1. Raised by paternal uncle - Muhammad (whose name means "highly praised") was born in 570 A.D. in Mecca. His father died before he was born, and his mother when he was six. For two years after that he was raised by his grandfather until he, too, died and his paternal uncle, Abu Talib, raised him in the city of Mecca.

2. Muhammad's marriage – At age 25 he married an older woman named Khadija, a wealthy caravan owner whose caravan he tended.

3. Muhammad's spiritual leanings – Muhammad often retired to a cave in the surrounding mountains to meditate and pursue his spiritual interests. He was troubled by the religious practices of the Meccans, especially because of the idolatry and immorality.

B. The Reading/Recitation

1. At age 40 Muhammad, in the month of Ramadan in 610 A.D., while in a cave on Hira, was visited by an angel *Jibril* (Gabriel), holding a scroll. Throughout the rest of his life Muhammad received further revelations. Believing these were, indeed, from God, Muhammad ensured that others wrote down the words he would utter. He often went into trances before uttering the words of the *Qur'an*

2. Allah is One, The chief message At the heart of the *Qur'an's* theology was that God is one, and has no partners or equals, and to believe that he does is the ultimate blasphemy.

C. The Conflict

Although Muhammad's influence was minor at first, more and more people listened and followed his teachings. As his following became larger, more visible and outspoken, the natives of Mecca began to see Muhammad, his teaching and his growing community/brotherhood (*umma*) as a threat and began persecuting them. In the year 622 A.D. Muhammad and his followers left Mecca and went about 280 miles north to *Yathrib* (later called *Medina*; "the city" of the Prophet), and there established Islam as a theocracy. There, the people were far more receptive and eager for Muhammad's message. This exodus from Mecca is called the *Hijrah* or "emigration" and marks the beginning of the Islamic calendar.

D. The Importance of Mecca

Despite his reception and success in Medina, Muhammad still wanted Mecca. The main reason for this was that the Kaaba was in Mecca, the location where, it was believed, Abraham offered Ishmael (not Isaac as the Bible states) to Allah in obedience, symbolizing the ultimate in submission (*islam*) to God.

III. The Qur'an

A. *Meaning and Arrangement* -

a. "Recitation" – The word *Qur'an* literally means "recitation" and refers to its being revealed to Muhammad and recited by him to be written down and read for all true followers of Allah.

b. 114 surahs (chapters) –

Muhammad with the Qur'an

IV. Core Theology and Practices of Islam

A. *Five Core Beliefs*

a. The oneness/unity of Allah –

b. The Prophets/Messengers of Islam with primacy on Muhammad -

c. The Scriptures with primacy on the Qur'an –

d. Angelic activity –

e. The Day of Resurrection and Final Judgment -

THINKING

"Both Christians and Muslims share belief in a sovereign Deity who is one, heavenly, spiritual, the creator of heaven and earth and the judge of all mankind. Christians call Him "*God*" and Muslims call Him "*Allah*". One may thus presume that the attributes of God and Allah are the same. A careful examination of the matter, however, will prove that it is not exactly so."

Abdullah Al Araby, *God of Christianity vs. Allah of Islam,* http://www.islamreview.com/articles/godvsallah.shtml July 2012

Question: Do Christians and Muslims worship the same god? Why or why not?

B. *The Five Pillars of Islam*

a. The Confession of Faith (*Shahada*) -

b. The Contact Prayers (*Salat*)

c. Alms or Poor Tax (*Zakat*) –

d. Fasting during Ramadan –

e. The Pilgrimage to Mecca (*Hajj*) –

V. Summarizing Islam's Plan of Salvation

A. *What is salvation?* – Entering Paradise on Judgment Day, and escaping Hell

B. *What makes salvation necessary?* – Humanity's forgetfulness/ignorance of Allah's Oneness and the Qur'an; and sure damnation if Allah is not remembered and obeyed.

C. *What makes salvation possible?* – Revelation of the *Qur'an* to Muhammad; it is called, among other things a "mercy" and a "guide' to humanity to find submission, the true religion.

D. *What makes salvation personal?* – Submission to Allah as demonstrated by strict adherence to the Five Pillars.

VI. Islam since Muhammad

Death of Muhammad and Division of Muslims

    a. *The Sunnis*

    b. *The Shiites*

The two major sects of Islam, Sunni and Shi.ite, were divided originally over a dispute as to who should serve as the first *caliph*, or successor, to Muhammad, who had failed to appoint one before his death. The Sunni Muslims insisted that Muhammad.s successor should be elected. The Shi.ite (or Shia.h) Muslims thought he should come through Muhammad's bloodline, which would have meant Ali, Muhammad's cousin and son-in-law, would be his successor.

VII. Some Biblical Perspective on Islam

Of the three faiths we have examined, Islam is closest to Christianity. In fact, the *Qur'an* even speaks very highly of Jesus, but while this is the case, it does not honor Jesus as God, which the Bible says, clearly, we are to do (John 5:23). Let's briefly examine this Jesus question, and demonstrate how Islam and Christianity are not teaching the same thing at all when it comes to the true worship of God and why this even matters.

In the *Qur'an, surah* 3:42-60 we find a very lengthy teaching about Jesus, much of which is consistent with the Gospels. His birth was preannounced to Mary, he was born of a virgin, He will be obeyed and teach obedience to the disciples (meaning they were Muslims, of course), he performed miracles like healing lepers, the blind and raising the dead! (a claim Muhammad could not make). Jesus was "faultless!" (v.19:19, another thing true about Jesus, but not Muhammad), and "a revelation" and a "mercy" and that all this was "ordained." (v.21) Jesus unlike any other messenger of Allah, was said to be "supported/strengthened . . . with the holy Spirit." (2:253, 5:110). Jesus alone, was given "the Gospel" (5:46, 57:27) . Jesus is regularly identified in the *Qur'an* as "Messiah" which no other prophet, including Muhammad, is designated.

# THINKING

Question: How do Muslims view the Christian Bible?

"The wide spectrum of variance in the attitude towards the Bible among Muslims comes in large part from a tension between what the Quran and Hadith teach about the Bible, and what the Bible teaches about Muslim doctrine. More specifically, the Quran and Hadith teach that Muslims should accept and read the *Taurat* (Torah) and the *Injeel* (Gospels) as authoritative revelation from God. The difficulty for Muslims is that they know (or have been told) that the Bible (especially the *Injeel*) contradicts Muslim doctrine by teaching things like the deity of Jesus, the Trinity, the crucifixion, and the resurrection. So in light of the many exhortations by Muhammad the Prophet of Islam to read and accept the *Taurat* and *Injeel* which are known to contradict the Quran, the Muslim logically arrives at the *apriori* conclusion that the *Taurat* and *Injeel* must have been corrupted since the time of the Prophet."

Joseph Alrasouli, Giving An Answer Muslim View of the Bible.
http://www.givingananswer.org/articles/muslimviewofbible.html , July 2012

Despite these amazingly positive, and even biblical things said about Jesus, the *Qur'an* denies two very central biblical teachings which happens to undermine the essence of Christianity. According to *surah* 4:157-158 Jesus was not crucified, but in a sleight of hand, Allah made it "appear" that the Jews had slain Jesus. Instead, Allah "took him up" to himself (although we don't know exactly what this means).

Messiah's/Christ's literal death is central to the Bible (Isaiah 53 and 1 Corinthians) and the heart of the gospel. Christianity is nothing without the crucifixion of Christ, and His unique resurrection "from the dead." More troubling, however, is the *Qur'an's* blatant denial of Jesus' deity. Of course this grows out of the doctrine of Allah's oneness, making it impossible that he could have equal "partners" in heaven. A related idea attacked by this is Jesus' being the "son" of God. According to the *Qur'an*, God cannot have a son (2:116, 4:171, 6:101) and that there is "no warrant" (10:68), for such a claim. To suggest this is "a disastrous thing" with potentially devastating cosmic effects (19:88-93). In fact, at some points Jesus, the Messiah, son of Mary (as the *Qur'an* frequently refers to him), is the very one who denies his own sonship and deity, pronouncing severe judgment on any who would suggest otherwise (5:72-3). It follows from this that Jesus was "no other than a messenger," indistinct from all previous messengers (2:136, 4:171), and nothing other than a human, just like Adam (3:59), which, of course, annuls any idea of Jesus' pre-existence. Jesus accepted his status as a mere "slave" of Allah (19:30, 33, 43:59; like we all should), and even predicts the coming of Muhammad, whose name would be "even more praised" (61:6) than his.

To answer this challenge we need to compare/contrast the biblical view of Jesus, and what He claimed about himself, to the Qur'an's depiction of Jesus. For sake of time, we will limit this analysis to the Gospel of John in which Jesus' deity is unequivocally proclaimed with a purpose to guide us into believing that He is the Christ, the son of God, and that believing we might have life in His name (John 20:31).

 **SCRIPTURE**

John 14:6 (KJV)
Jesus saith unto him, I am the way, the truth, and the life: no man cometh unto the Father, but by me.
John 1:1-2 (NLT)
In the beginning the Word already existed. The Word was with God, and the Word was God.
He existed in the beginning with God.
John 1:14 (NLT)
So the Word became human and made his home among us. He was full of unfailing love and faithfulness. And we have seen his glory, the glory of the Father's one and only Son.
Colossians 1:16 (NLT)
For by him were all things created, that are in heaven, and that are in earth, visible and invisible, whether [they be] thrones, or dominions, or principalities, or powers: all things were created by him, and for him:

In John's "prologue," Jesus is clearly identified as the pre-existing, eternal, Word, equivalent with God (1:1-2,). The Word was the agent of creation of all things, including the world (1:3, 10 see also Colossians 1:16-17 and Hebrews 1:2). The eternal Word which dwelt with God and was God and which created all things was "made flesh and dwelt among us" and was the "son" who made the Father known to the world during his earthly sojourn (1:18, see also Colossians 1:19, 2:9 and Hebrews 1:3). This remarkable passage has already established Jesus' pre-existence, His equality with God, His being the creator of all things, and His sonship, making known "the Father" to the world; all things denied by the Qur'an. The rest of John's gospel clearly establishes Jesus' sonship and deity, and that this is the critical issue for humans to believe so that they might, be forgiven of their sins, and have eternal life.

The self-understanding of Jesus we find in the Bible is clearly poles apart from that which we see in the *Qur'an*. As we have seen, in the gospel of John alone Jesus explicitly claims to be the "Son of God" (which is equivalent to a claim to deity), and to have pre-existed with the "Father" "in heaven" prior to His appearance on earth. He claims to have "come from heaven" and not to have originated in the world like all humans, He asserts his sinlessness, and how this qualifies His doctrine as authoritative and certifies his oneness with God. He also predicts his literal death and its purpose, and explains that he, as God alone, has the power to forgive sins. Jesus Christ and His message about Himself as the Son of God and the one in whom we must place our saving faith is all that matters.

COMPARISON CHART: ISLAM AND CHRISTIANITY

BELIEF	ISLAM	CHRISTIANITY
God	Only one god - called Allah	Only one God - a triune being called God or Yahweh
Jesus	A prophet who was virgin-born, but not the Son of God	Divine son of God who was virgin-born. He is God's Word and Savior to humanity
Crucifixion	Jesus was not crucified. Someone was substituted for Jesus and He hid until He could meet with the disciples	A fact of history that is necessary for the atonement of sin and the salvation of believers
Jesus' Resurrection	Since Muslims do not believe in the Crucifixion, there is no need to believe in the Resurrection	A fact of history that signifies God's victory over sin and death
Trinity	A blasphemy signifying belief in three gods. In Islam, the Trinity is mistakenly thought to be God, Jesus, and Mary	The one God is eternally revealed in three coequal and coeternal persons: God the Father, God the Son, and God the Holy Spirit
Salvation	Salvation is achieved by submitting to the will of Allah. There is no assurance of salvation - it is granted by Allah's mercy alone	Salvation is a gift accepted by faith in the atonement of Jesus Christ on the Cross and provided through God's grace
Bible	Muslims accept the Bible (especially the Pentateuch, Psalms, and Gospels) insofar as it agrees with the Qur'an	The Bible is the inspired Word of God that is complete and not to be added to
Qur'an (Koran)	A later revelation that supersedes and corrects errors in the Bible	Not accepted as divine revelation
Muhammad	The last in the line of prophets and, therefore, the final authority in spiritual matters	Not accepted as a prophet or legitimate theological source
Angels	These divine messengers are created from light and are not worshipped. Satan is a fallen angel	Angels are defined in the Bible as heavenly servants of God who act as His messengers
Last Days	There will be bodily resurrection and final judgment with final destination. All Muslims go to heaven, though some must be purged of their sins first. All infidels are destined for hell	There will be bodily resurrection in the last days. Final judgment and eternal destination (heaven or hell) will be decided based on acceptance of Jesus as Savior and His removal of the sin which separates each person from God

By NSRK Ravi   http://www.4truth.net/fourtruthpbworld.aspx?pageid=8589953009

SALVATION COMPARISON CHART

	Islam	Buddhism	Hinduism	Christianity
WHAT IS SALVATION?	Being **rewarded** on Judgment Day with entrance into Paradise if one's righteous deeds are determined to outweigh their sinful deeds	Achievement of *Nirvana* – "**Cessation**" of desire and the suffering that comes from desire, including the cycles of death and rebirth.	Achievement of *Moksha* - "**Liberation**" from the painful cycle of death and rebirth. **Realization** of one's unity with Ultimate Reality (*Brahman*)	Being **rescued** from sin's eternal consequences, temporal control and actual condition. **Receiving** eternal life as **a gift of grace**
WHAT MAKES SALVATION NECESSARY?	Humans are ignorant of their true nature as a Muslim (submitter) and destined for Hell's fire until they submit to Allah's will	Humans are **enslaved** by *karma* to *samsara* **because of** their **desire** for the impermanent things of this world, and experience endless **suffering** due to this.	Humans, because of *karma*, are trapped in the cycle of death and rebirth (*samsara*) because of their **ignorance** of Ultimate Reality, and attachment to worldly illusion (*maya*)	Humans are **sinful**, and are **separated** from and **subject to the eternal wrath** of a Holy and Righteous God
WHAT MAKES SALVATION POSSIBLE?	The *Qur'an* which teaches humans of their true identity as Muslims who must willingly submit to the will of Allah.	The enlightenment, **example and teachings of Siddhartha Gautama** who became the Buddha through overcoming his desire.	The **knowledge** found in the Hindu Scriptures about escaping *karma* and *samsara* and achieving *moksha* and one's ultimate unity with *Brahman*.	*Divine initiative:* God through **love** and **grace** reveals the **gospel** and provides to rescue humans from sin through the substitutionary **death and resurrection of Jesus Christ.**
WHAT MAKES SALVATION PERSONAL?	*Human Effort:* **Confessing** the *Shahada*; believing the **Articles of Faith** and practicing the **Five Pillars of Islam**.	*Human Effort:* Accepting the **Four Noble Truths** and following the **Noble Eightfold Path.** Taking refuge in the Buddha, *Dhamma* (his teachings) and *Sangha* (community of fellow Buddhists).	*Human effort:* Becoming a **yogi** (one who practices yoga, a discipline by which can realize oneness with Ultimate Reality); **Living faithfully** to one's given station in life (*caste* and *dharma*).	**Repentance** and **faith;** Owning up to and turning from one's sin and turning to the Savior, Jesus Christ, alone for salvation and submitting to him as the Lord.
WHAT IS THE RELATIONSHIP BETWEEN SALVATION AND MORALITY?	**Salvation** (earning Paradise) possible only **through faithfully living a moral life** as defined by *Qur'an* and *Sunnah* to be determined on Judgment Day.	**Salvation is the result of** rigorously living **a moral life** as articulated in the Noble Eightfold Path and the Five precepts (Ten precepts if a monk or nun).	Salvation (*moksha*) **is the result of a moral life**, but especially being a yogi and following the discipline of yoga to focus in union with Brahman.	The **moral life is the result of salvation**. When one receives Christ they are empowered through the Holy spirit to live as they ought to and to please God by following Jesus' moral example.

Chapter Nine – Islam (Religious Worldview)

Chapter Ten

RELATIVISM
Affirming a Biblical Worldview

John 3:19-21 - *"And this is the condemnation, that the light has come into the world, and men loved darkness rather than light, because their deeds were evil. For everyone practicing evil hates the light and does not come to the light, lest his deeds should be exposed. But he who does the truth comes to the light, that his deeds may be clearly seen, that they have been done in God."*

Judges 17:6 – *"In those days there was no king in Israel; everyone did what was right in his own eyes."*

I. Relative Trust and Absolute Truth

Relative Truth – "Truth that is true at only <u>one time</u> and at <u>one place</u>. It's true to <u>some people</u> and not to others. It's true <u>now</u> but it may not have been true in the past and it may not be again in the future, <u>it's always subject to change</u>. It is also subject to the perspective of people."

Absolute Truth – "Whatever is true at <u>one time</u> and at <u>one place</u> is true at all times and at all places. What is true for one person is <u>true for all</u> persons. Truth is true whether we believe it or not. <u>Truth is discovered or it is revealed</u>, it is not invented by a culture or by religious men."   *(Taken from Absolutism verses Relativism http://www.letusreason.org/Apolo1.htm , 2009)*

II. Three Relativistic Views:

 **BIOGRAPHY**

A. _____ Relativism

   1. People and propositions

     a. Ruth Benedict – (*Patterns of Culture*, Houghton Mifflin, 1989)

"We recognize that morality differs in every society and is a convenient term for socially approved habits. Mankind has always preferred to say, 'it is morally good,' rather than 'it is

Ruth Benedict, née Ruth Fulton - (born June 5, 1887, New York, N.Y., U.S.—died Sept. 17, 1948, New York City), American anthropologist whose theories had a profound influence on <u>cultural anthropology</u>, especially in the area of <u>culture</u> and personality.
Ruth Benedict. (2012). In *Encyclopædia Britannica*. Retrieved from http://www.britannica.com/EBchecked/topic/60482/Ruth-Benedict

Chapter Ten - Relativism

habitual' . . . but historically the two phrases are synonymous"

b. Cultural relativism is an _____ approach which states that all cultures are of equal value . . . what is bad in one culture may not be bad in another. What is good in one culture may not be good in another.

2. Principles
   a. The fact of _____ between the morals of cultures is undeniable.
   b. Individual and societal morals are _____ by _____ tradition.
   c. No moral absolutes exist.
   d. _____ is the only acceptable response.

3. Summary of Problems with this philosophy
   a. The disagreement between cultures is overstated.
   b. You can _____ any moral behavior (ie; Holocaust, genocide, slavery, rape, child abuse & pornography etc)
   c. The conclusion does not follow from the premise.
      1)
      2) _____ (or lack of it) does not destroy objective truth.
   d. It is neither uneducated nor ignorant to insist that morality may be OBJECTIVE (and consequently universal and absolute) rather than relative to culture or individuals.
   e. A cultural relativist denies that we can know what God's moral will is for all people. But . . . Matthew 28:19.

> **THINKING**
>
> "There have been differences between . . . moralities, but these have never amounted to anything like a total difference. If anyone will take the trouble to compare the moral teachings of say, the ancient Egyptians, Babylonians, Hindus, Chinese, Greeks and Romans, what will really strike him will be how very like they are to each other, and to our own."
>
> Lewis, C.S.
> Mere Christianity,
> Harper 2001

Chapter Ten - Relativism

B. _____ Relativism (Subjectivism)

1. People and Propositions

    a. Protagoras – "Man is the measure of all things"

    b. David Hume – "Take any action allow'd to be vicious […] The vice entirely escapes you, as long as you consider the object. You never can find it, till you turn your reflection into your own breast, and find a sentiment of disapprobation (disapproval), which arises in you, towards this action. Here is a matter of fact; but `tis the object of feeling, not of reason…" (Hume, 1751, 9.6)

BIOGRAPHY

David Hume, (born May 7 [April 26, Old Style], 1711, Edinburgh, Scot.—died Aug. 25, 1776, Edinburgh), Scottish philosopher, historian, economist, and essayist, known especially for his philosophical empiricism and skepticism.

Hume conceived of philosophy as the inductive, experimental science of human nature. Taking the scientific method of the English physicist Sir Isaac Newton as his model and building on the epistemology of the English philosopher John Locke, Hume tried to describe how the mind works in acquiring what is called knowledge. He concluded that no theory of reality is possible; there can be no knowledge of anything beyond experience. Despite the enduring impact of his theory of knowledge, Hume seems to have considered himself chiefly as a moralist.

David Hume. (2012). In *Encyclopædia Britannica*. Retrieved from http://www.britannica.com/EBchecked/topic/276139/David-Hume

2. Principle

    a. Morality is a matter of _____.
    - If you _____ after doing something, it is _____ for you.
    - If you feel _____ after doing something it is _____ for you.

    b. No one can judge another person for doing wrong. Two people can define truth in totally conflicting ways and both are _____. "… *truth is something that is truth to the individual because perceptions are different, people are different, minds are different.*"

    - New Age Therapist

    c. "There are no Absolutes"

3. Summary of Problems with this philosophy

    a. "There are no absolutes" is an absolute.

    b. Two opposing views cannot be both right at the same time.

    c. The moment a relativist tries to get you to believe their position they have _____ their position.

d. Generally, people want to live by a _____ morality but want to be _____ according to an _____ morality.

e. Denying God and moral absolutes is often a strategy for guilt free permissiveness. (John 3:19)

C. _____ Relativism

1. Principles

   a. Humans are social animals, therefore morality is a matter of social, not individual, concern.

   b. The only measures of what is right and wrong are the _____ _____.

   c. The _____ rules

2. Summary of Problems with this philosophy

   a. If socially approved morality cannot be criticized, then:
      1) It is meaningless to speak of or strive for social moral improvement.
      2) Criticism of any practice of any other culture is unjustifiable.

   b. One may be a member of two "societies" with opposing views, making some acts both right and wrong.

   c. _____.

```
                        RELATIVISM
           /                |                \
  CULTURAL         SUBJECTIVISM        CONVENTIONALISM
  RELATIVISM       Morality is a       Morality is a
  Since cultures   Factor dependent    Factor dependent
  Vary in their    Upon individual     Upon Social
  Moral beliefs    Choice and          Convention (51%
  It follows that no  Preference.      morality)
  Universal moral
  Principles exist
```

Chapter Ten - Relativism

Chapter Eleven

TELEOLOGICAL ETHICS
Affirming a Biblical Worldview

Psalm 119:1-2 (NLT) - *"Happy are people of integrity, who follow the law of the LORD Happy are those who obey his decrees and search for him with all their hearts."*

II Timothy 3:1-5 (NLT) - *You should also know this, Timothy, that in the last days there will be very difficult times. 2 For people will love only themselves and their money. They will be boastful and proud, scoffing at God, disobedient to their parents, and ungrateful. They will consider nothing sacred. 3 They will be unloving and unforgiving; they will slander others and have no self-control; they will be cruel and have no interest in what is good. 4 They will betray their friends, be reckless, be puffed up with pride, and love pleasure rather than God. 5 They will act as if they are religious, but they will reject the power that could make them godly. You must stay away from people like that.*

I. Primary Idea:

All teleological theories focus upon the results/ends of an act to determine the morality of that act. They differ as to which results are to be sought.

Teleology and Ethics

Teleological moral systems are characterized primarily by a focus on the **consequences** which any action might have (for that reason, they are often referred to as consequentalist moral systems, and both terms are used here). Thus, in order to make correct moral choices, we have to have some **understanding of what will result** from our choices. When we make choices which result in the correct consequences, then we are acting morally; when we make choices which result in the incorrect consequences, then we are acting immorally.
(http://atheism.about.com/library/FAQs/phil/blfaq_phileth_sys.htm)

Deontology and Ethics

Deontological moral systems are characterized primarily by a focus upon adherence to independent **moral rules or duties**. Thus, in order to make the correct moral choices, we simply have to **understand what our moral duties** are and what correct rules exist which regulate those duties. <u>When we follow our duty, we are behaving morally</u>. When we fail to follow our duty, we are behaving immorally.

(http://atheism.about.com/library/FAQs/phil/blfaq_phileth_sys.htm)

Note: The Biblical/Christian Worldview is often characterized as a deontological approach to moral decision-making. However, a pure deontological approach can lead to legalism. A true Biblical/Christian Worldview approach to morality is more closely associated with the Spirit filled Life (Galatians 5:16).

Galatians 5:16-18 (KJV)
I say then, Walk in the Spirit, and ye shall not fulfil the lust of the flesh. For the flesh lusteth against the Spirit, and the Spirit against the flesh: and these are contrary the one to the other: so that ye cannot do the things that ye would.
But if ye be led of the Spirit, ye are not under the law.

II. Four Teleological Approaches to Ethics

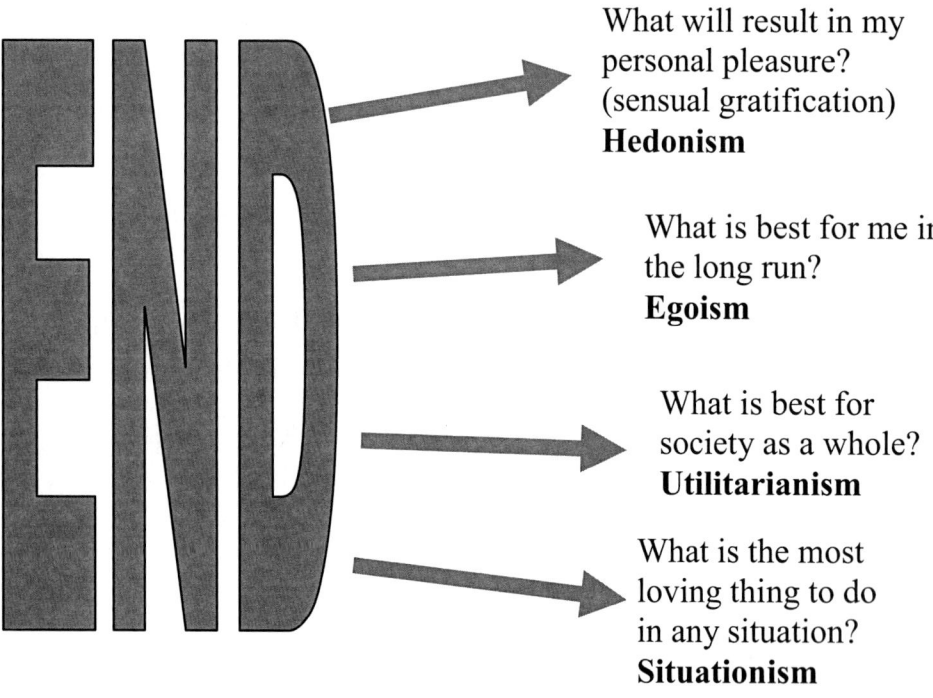

What will result in my personal pleasure? (sensual gratification)
Hedonism

What is best for me in the long run?
Egoism

What is best for society as a whole?
Utilitarianism

What is the most loving thing to do in any situation?
Situationism

A. **SENSUAL HEDONISM** - (Sensual gratification should be the goal of all actions)

1. Principal Idea

   An act is right if and only if it maximizes my pleasure and minimizes my pain.

2. Prominent Person

   Epicurus - Greek philosopher.

3. Problems

   - Often grows out of a nihilistic view of life - (1Corinthians15:32). It is thus more of an escape mentality than a morality - (Proverbs 14:13).
   - Commits the naturalistic fallacy.
   - Usually ends up violating the law of non-contradiction. By the unbridled exercise of our freedom, we enslave ourselves.
   - Is subject to the hedonistic paradox which states that *the surest way to miss pleasure in life is to seek it as an end in itself* - (i.e. make it one's primary goal - Ecclesiastes 2:1-11; 5:10).

BIOGRAPHY

Epicurus, (born 341 BC, died 270, Athens), Greek philosopher, author of an ethical philosophy of simple pleasure, friendship, and retirement. His philosophy was not about choosing what was morally right, but rather, what action – whether limited or promoted – results in the most pleasure.
Epicurus. (2012). In *Encyclopædia Britannica*. Retrieved from http://www.britannica.com/EBchecked/topic/189746/Epicurus

BIOGRAPHY

Ayn Rand, original name Alissa Zinovievna Rosenbaum (born 1905, died1982), Russian-born American writer best known for her successful novels promoting individualism and laissez-faire capitalism. In an appendix to *Atlas Shrugged*, **Rand** described her systematic philosophy, which she called objectivism, as "in essence…the concept of man as a heroic being, with his own happiness as the moral purpose of his life, with productive achievement as his noblest activity, and reason as his only absolute."
Ayn Rand. (2012). In *Encyclopædia Britannica*. Retrieved from http://www.britannica.com/EBchecked/topic/490984/Ayn-Rand

B. **RATIONAL HEDONISM** - (Egoism - Self-interest or personal happiness should be the goal of all actions).

1. Principal Idea

   Since humans are naturally selfish, i.e. always act selfishly, it follows that an act is right if and only if it is done to benefit the one acting. (selfishness is seen as virtue).

2. Prominent Person

   Ayn Rand - American Philosopher

3. Problems

- The premise is <u>impossible</u> to prove (How can one say all humans always act selfishly?)
- Commits the <u>naturalistic</u> fallacy.
- It robs relationships of the warmth and "love" that make them meaningful by making every act one for <u>personal gain</u>, not caring about others.
- Is self-defeating (contradictory) to teach this to others as true may not be in one's <u>best interests</u>.
- Commits the <u>either/or</u> fallacy. Falsely states that morality involves either exclusively caring for oneself, or exclusively caring for others at the expense of oneself.
- <u>The Bible</u> teaches otherwise; genuine concern for others is not <u>incompatible</u> with a healthy self-interest - (Cf. Proverbs 11:17; Matthew 22:40).

C. <u>UTILITARIANISM</u> - (The <u>common good</u> should be the goal of all actions)

1. Principal Idea

   Since humans are social beings by nature, it follows that selfishness is not right. An act is right if and only if it results in **the greatest happiness/benefit/good for the greatest number of people.** (Social hedonism).

2. Prominent People

   Jeremy Bentham, John Stuart Mill

To Bentham maximizing happiness comes from promoting pleasure and minimizing pain. He suggests seven categories:

(1) **Intensity**: How intense is the pleasure?

(2) **Duration**: How long does the pleasure last?

(3) **Certainty**: How certain are you that the pleasure will occur?

(4) **Proximity**: How soon will the pleasure be experienced?

(5) **Fecundity**: How many more pleasures will result from this one?

(6) **Purity**: How free from pain is the pleasure?

(7) **Extent**: How many people will experience the pleasure?

3. Problems
   - Commits the **naturalistic fallacy**.
   - Since "happiness" is defined differently by people, whose definition should we use?
   - It is impossible to calculate. Are the majority really happy, how could we possibly know?
   - Has historically led to many injustices and violations of human rights for the sake of "the common good."
   - "The needs of the many outweigh the needs of the few or the one." Mr. Spock

D. **SITUATIONISM/SITUATION ETHICS** (The most loving thing should be the goal of all actions)

1. Principal Idea
   To love is the highest good, therefore an act is right if and only if it reflects the most loving thing you can do in any situation, even if it means breaking traditional moral rules (like the Ten Commandments) to do it.

 **BIOGRAPHY**

Joseph Francis Fletcher (1905-1991) was a philosopher widely recognized for his work in moral theory and applied ethics. Best known for the method of consequentialist moral reasoning espoused in his book *Situation Ethics*. He proclaimed that human beings are more important than moral rules and that appraisal of consequences rather than rules should guide moral decision making.
Read more:
http://www.answers.com/topic/joseph-fletcher#ixzz20F2gt3F9

2. Prominent Person
   Joseph Fletcher

3. Problems
   - To say that love supersedes all other commandments is a gross misinterpretation of scripture (Cf. Romans 13:8-10). Love fulfills, it does not annul, the law. Love and law are not mutually exclusive ideas. The law shows us how to apply love.

- Ignores the possibility that God's commands may be given for our <u>good</u>, and are thus a product of His wisdom and <u>love</u> for us. (Deuteronomy. 10:12-13; Psalm 119:1-2; John 13:17).
- Like all teleological theories, it mistakenly assumes that we can either know or calculate what will be the best for <u>all neighbors</u> involved.

Note:

Norman Geisler's view of Fletcher's Situational Ethics and application of Graded Absolutism.

"Fletcher believes that the situation determines what one should do in a given case; graded absolutism holds that situational factors only help one to discover what God has determined that we should do. That is, the situation does not fill an empty absolute with content and thereby determine what one should do. Rather, the situational factors merely help one discover which command of God is applicable to that particular case." (Geisler, p123)

"…in Graded Absolutism the Christian does not decide for himself what the ethical priorities are. It is God who establishes the pyramid of values in accordance with His own nature. These are recorded in Scripture and, hence, they are no more subjective than is anything else revealed in Scripture. The priority of values is objective and determined by God; the only subjective factor is our understanding and acceptance of God's values. But this is a limitation shared by the other Christian views as well." (Geisler, p124)

Geisler, Norman L. *Christian Ethics*. Grand Rapids: Baker Books, 2000.

Chapter Twelve

DETERMINISM
Affirming a Biblical Worldview

Joshua 24:15 (KJV) *And if it seem evil unto you to serve the LORD, <u>choose</u> you this day whom ye will serve; whether the gods which your fathers served that [were] on the other side of the flood, or the gods of the Amorites, in whose land ye dwell: but as for me and my house, we will serve the LORD.*

Proverbs 1:29 (NLT) – *For they hated knowledge and <u>chose</u> not to fear the LORD.*

Romans 14:12-13 (NLT) - *Yes, each of us will have to give a personal account to God. So don't condemn each other anymore. Decide instead to live in such a way that you will not put an obstacle in another Christian's path.*

I. Primary Idea:

No actions are _____ chosen, but are the results of specific, traceable _____, whether these be hereditary, environmental, cultural or biochemical.

   A. **Degrees/Levels** of Determinism:

      1. _____ Determinism.

         a. The _____ view that the future is governed by forces upon which we have no control or recourse. It is _____ to happen.

         b. Albert Einstein stated in a speech in 1932, *"Human beings in their thinking, feeling and acting are not free but are as causally bound as the stars in their motions"* (Einstein 2007, 205)

      2. _____ Determinism.

         a. Soft determinism, is less harsh in it's rhetoric but still consistent in the final outcome.

         b. Soft determinism is sometimes called "compatibilism" since it tries to be compatible with free choice by allowing the input of facts, knowledge and yet still insist that the future is determined by the past. This position is defended by making knowledge itself one of the antecedent causes. Thus all is still determined.

c. As the German philosopher Arthur Schopenhauer said, *"A man can do as he wills, but not will as he wills."*

B. **Types** of Determinism.

1. **Environmental** Determinism.

    a. A person's environment is the conditioning antecedent cause of the behavior. What part does nurture and conditioning (see B.F Skinner and Behaviorism) play in human development?

    b. Does the external force of a conditioning environment and a learning experience determine the action and outcome itself, or can an individual exercise the will to choose, noting that the choice may, or may not, align with their environmental conditioning? (Eph 4:6)

> **SCRIPTURE**
>
> I Corinthians 15:12-14 (NLT)
> But tell me this—since we preach that Christ rose from the dead, why are some of you saying there will be no resurrection of the dead?
> For if there is no resurrection of the dead, then Christ has not been raised either.
> And if Christ has not been raised, then all our preaching is useless, and your faith is useless.
>
> I Corinthians 15:12-14 (NLT)
> But tell me this—since we preach
> And what value was there in fighting wild beasts—those people of Ephesus [fn]—if there will be no resurrection from the dead? And if there is

2. **Biological** or **Genetic** Determinism.

    a. DNA

    b. Everything from criminality, addictive disorders, personality traits, and behavior patterns (both positive and negative) are portrayed less as a matter of choice and more as genetic destiny.

3. **Theistic** Determinism.

    a. Theistic determinism is "the view that God ordains every event and situation; man does not have capacity to choose or influence his own ultimate destiny"

    (Geisler 1993, 205).

    b. The Theistic determinist argues that God is the first cause and everything must be known by Him, in order for Him to remain omniscient. A Theistic determinist also believes that everything must be determined by Him, in order for Him to remain sovereign.

c. "It is true that everything God knows must occur according to his will. If it did not, then God would be wrong in what he knew. For an omniscient Mind cannot be wrong in what it knows. However, it does not follow from this that all events are determined (i.e., caused by God). God could simply determine that we be self-determining beings in a moral sense." (Geisler 1999, 197)

II. People and Propositions

A. Baron Paul d'Holbach (1723-1789) - "Man's life is a line that nature commands him . . . Without him ever being able to swerve from it even for an instant . . . he is good or bad, happy or miserable, wise or foolish, reasonable or irrational, without his will counting for anything in these various states."
   (Baron Paul d'Holbach, *System of Nature*, 1770)

B. Clarence Darrow (1857-1938)

BIOGRAPHY

Clarence Darrow (born 1857—died 1938) A lawyer whose work as defense counsel in many dramatic criminal trials earned him a place in American legal history. He is often remember d for closing remarks in the case where he saved (1924) Richard Loeb and Nathan Leopold from a death sentence (though not from imprisonment) for the murder of 14-year-old Robert Franks in Chicago.
Clarence Darrow. (2012). In *Encyclopædia Britannica*. Retrieved from http://www.britannica.com/EBchecked/topic/151820/Clarence-Darrow

C. Albert Einstein (1879-1955) – "Everything is determined, the beginning as well as the end, by  forces over which we have no control. It is determined for insects as well as for the stars. Human beings, vegetables or cosmic dust, we all dance to a mysterious tune, intoned in the distance by an invisible piper."
   Einstein, Albert. Speech- Spinoza Society of America, 1932. Quoted in Walter Isaacson, Einstein: His Life and Universe. New York: Simon & Schuster, 2007.

D. B. F. Skinner (1904-1990) - American philosopher, the Father of Behaviorism

"In what we may call the pre-scientific view a person's behavior is at least to some extent his own achievement. He is free to deliberate, decide, act, possibly in original ways, and he is to be given credit for his successes and blamed for his failures. In the scientific view . . . . . . a person's behavior is determined by a genetic endowment traceable to the evolutionary history of the species and by the environmental circumstances to which as an individual he has been exposed." As we learn more about the effects of the environment, we have less reason to attribute any part of human behavior to an autonomous controlling agent."
   Skinner, B.F. *Beyond Freedom and Dignity*, 1971 p.101

Chapter Twelve - Determinism

III. Principles

A. Every _____, _____ or _____ can be traced back to some natural, antecedent cause.

B. Antecedent causes of all human behavior are found in _____, _____, _____, and _____ factors.

C. All our motives, desires, and beliefs are traceable to these determining factors.

D. Since all actions are caused, none are truly _____. Freedom is a "subjective illusion" man holds about himself.

E. Since moral responsibility is based on the premise that our actions are freely chosen, moral responsibility is fiction, not a fact.

F. All human actions are predictable, controllable and manipulable if the antecedent causes can be discovered.

G. All human and natural history can be understood as a cosmic domino effect.

IV. Pertinence

A. Crime and criminals

"There is no such thing as a crime as the word is generally understood. I do not believe there is any sort of distinction between . . . the people in and out of jails . . . I do not believe that people are in jail because they deserve to be. They are in jail simply because they can not avoid it on account of circumstances entirely beyond their control and for which they are in no way responsible." (Clarence Darrow, *Crime and Criminals*, 1902)

B. The rise of "_____" and the "abuse excuse".

"Victimism has gained so much influence that as far as society is concerned, there is practically no such thing as sin anymore. Anyone can escape responsibility for his or her wrong doing simply by claiming the status of a victim. – (John F. McArthur Jr., *The Vanishing Conscience*, 1994)

Chapter Twelve - Determinism

C. _____, _____, and _____ which allow me to shift blame and deny responsibility for my own actions.

D. Genetic factors predispose us to certain behaviors. "The DNA made me do it"

V. Problems

A. Does not account for and cannot predict actions which careful _____ or _____ about alternative opinions.

B. People have been able to consciously and deliberately overcome conditioning factors of the past.

C. Human existence and experience cannot be adequately accounted for by a simple appeal to physical or external data.

D. Ultimately robs man of any kind of dignity, _____ or design.

E. The only consistent moral conclusion to be drawn from pure determinism is ethical nihilism which is a completely unlivable outlook on life.

F. Unfairly _____ groups of people as being drawn to these kinds of behaviors.

G. Threatens the _____ and _____ of society by sending a false message to victims (essentially all people) that disrespect and violence will be understood and pardoned.

H. The _____ becomes increasingly irrelevant in a society that focuses on sickness and circumstances rather than sin and guilt and the need for treatment and recovery rather than truth and repentance.

THINKING

Question: Does GOD determine everything that happens?

Question: In light of your above answer what part might God play in tragedies (Cancer, accidents, weather)?

Question: How would you respond to this statement: "Everything happens for a reason"?

Question: What is God's will for your life? Is this predetermined by GOD? What does it mean?

Recommended Reading: *Decision Making and the Will of God* by Garry Friesen (Multnomah Press)

Chapter Twelve - Determinism

Chapter Twelve - Determinism

Chapter Thirteen

NIHILISM

Affirming a Biblical Worldview

Genesis 1:26 (KJV) - *And God said, Let us make man in our image, after our likeness: and let them have dominion over the fish of the sea, and over the fowl of the air, and over the cattle, and over all the earth, and over every creeping thing that creepeth upon the earth.*

Psalm 139:14 (KJV) - *I will praise thee; for I am fearfully [and] wonderfully made: marvelous [are] thy works; and [that] my soul knoweth right well.*

Romans 8:38-39 (KJV) - *For I am persuaded, that neither death, nor life, nor angels, nor principalities, nor powers, nor things present, nor things to come, (39) Nor height, nor depth, nor any other creature, shall be able to separate us from the love of God, which is in Christ Jesus our Lord.*

I. Primary Idea:

* from the Latin meaning "nothing". (we use the root word to form the term annihilate which means to bring to nothing, or destroy)

In a universe void of _____ or any _____, there exists no real _____, _____ or _____ anywhere and humanity is on an irreversible, downward spiral into extinction.

II. People and Propositions

A. _____ (1844-1900)

German philosopher and writer

- "A Nihilist is the man who says of the world as it is, that it ought not to exist, and of the world as it ought to be, that it does not exist."

(Friedrich Nietzsche, *The Will To Power*, 1901)

BIOGRAPHY

Friedrich Nietzsche (1844 – 1900. German classical scholar, philosopher, and critic of culture. His attempts to unmask the motives that underlie traditional Western religion, morality, and philosophy deeply affected generations of theologians, philosophers, psychologists, poets, novelists, and playwrights. He thought through the consequences of the triumph of the Enlightenment's secularism, expressed in his observation that "God is dead," in a way that determined the agenda for many of Europe's most celebrated intellectuals after his death.
Friedrich Nietzsche. (2012). In *Encyclopædia Britannica*. Retrieved from http://www.britannica.com/EBchecked/topic/414670/Friedrich-Nietzsche

- *"Whither is God" he cried. "I shall tell you. We have killed him - you and I. All of us are his murderers.* - (Friedrich Nietzsche, *The Gay Science*, 1882)

B. _____ (1913-1960)

- *"There is but one truly philosophical problem, and that is suicide. Judging whether life is or is not worth living amounts to answering the fundamental question of philosophy"*

(Albert Camus, *The Myth of Sisyphus*, 1942)

C. _____ - (1872-1970) English Philosopher

- *"That Man is <u>the product of causes which had no prevision of the end they were achieving;</u> that his origin, his growth, his hopes and fears, his loves and beliefs, are but <u>the outcome of accidental collocations of atoms</u>: that no fire, no heroism, no intensity of thought and feeling, can preserve an individual life beyond the grave; that <u>all labours of the ages, all the devotion, all the inspiration, . . . Are destined to extinction in the vast death of the solar system</u>, and that the whole temple of Man's achievement must inevitably be <u>buried beneath the debris of a universe in ruins</u> - all these things, if not quite beyond dispute, are yet so nearly certain, that no philosophy, which rejects them, can hope to stand."*

(A Free Man's Worship" in Selected Papers of Bertrand Russell [New York: The Modern Library, 1927])

III. Principles

A. There is no _____

B. Man has no special _____.

C. Our actions, though thought to be free are actually predetermined by antecedent causes. (Man is a machine) Nihilism is the ultimate result of _____

D. We are helpless in a universe winding down into final nothingness.

SCRIPTURE

Ephesians 6:4 (KJV)
And, ye fathers, provoke not your children to wrath: but bring them up in the nurture and admonition of the Lord.

II Corinthians 5:17 (NLT)
This means that anyone who belongs to Christ has become a new person. The old life is gone; a new life has begun!

Ephesians 4:22-24 (NLT)
That ye put off concerning the former conversation the old man, which is corrupt according to the deceitful lusts;
And be renewed in the spirit of your mind;
And that ye put on the new man, which after God is created in righteousness and true holiness.

Chapter Thirteen - Nihilism

E. Life is absurd and has no purpose, meaning, value or final answers.

F. Any notion of evolution, progress or advancement is fictitious and delusional.

G. Once mankind realizes this they will respond in either utter despair, suicide or "recovery" which entails imagining (pretending) that somehow life has meaning.

IV. Pertinence

A. Toy Story – Buzz Lightyear discovers that he really has no cosmic significance and is nothing but a mere toy, a play thing of forces beyond his control and unaffected by his actions.

B. Many philosophical references in modern music. consider groups like Eminem *If I had*, Bad Religion *Against the Grain*, Pink Floyd *Another Brick in the Wall*, Marilyn Manson *Posthuman & Mechanical Animals* and Green Day *Insomniac*

C. Example from Art.

V. The Answer to Nihilism

A. Gen 1:26 – We are created in the image of God and therefore have value
(John 3:16, Matt 6:24-34, Matt 18:11-14)

B. Ps 139 – We are fearfully and wonderfully made…

C. Phil 4:4 "Rejoice in the Lord always…. v.7-8 …"think on these things

D. Through Christ we have the victory!
1. Sin – Rom 6:6
2. Life – Rom 8:35-39
3. Death – Jn 5:24,

E. The church will not cease to exist because of humanity's skepticism or disbelief.
Matthew 16:18 I Thessalonians 4:13-18

THINKING

Results of Nilhilism: Despair, Disillusionment, Denial, Depravity

Question: Read passages in the biblical book of Ecclesiastes written by Solomon. Was he a Nihilist, or as I call him a "recovering Hedonist"?

Question: what relationship might Hedonism have with Nihilism…and why?

Question: How might a nihilistic philosophy impact the Christian life?

Chapter Thirteen - Nihilism

Chapter Thirteen - Nihilism

TOLERANCE
Affirming a Biblical Worldview

I Peter 3:15 (KJV) - *But sanctify the Lord God in your hearts: and [be] ready always to [give] an answer to every man that asketh you a reason of the hope that is in you with meekness and fear:*

Romans 12:18 (KJV) *If it be possible, as much as lieth in you, live peaceably with all men.*

Romans 1:15-16 (KJV) *So, as much as in me is, I am ready to preach the gospel to you that are at Rome also. (16) For I am not ashamed of the gospel of Christ: for it is the power of God unto salvation to every one that believeth; to the Jew first, and also to the Greek.*

Tolerance Defined:

Note: To tolerate implies that we disagree. We don't "tolerate" people or ideas that share our views because there is nothing to "put up with".

DEFINITION

Webster's defines **tolerate** as "to recognize and respect [other's beliefs, practices, etc.] without sharing them," and "to bear or put up with [someone or something not especially liked].

I. Two Kinds of Tolerance:

A. Traditional

1. _____, even those with whom you disagree and those who are different from you.

2. Listening to and learning from other _____, cultures, and backgrounds.

3. Living peaceably alongside others, in spite of differences.

4. Accepting other people, regardless of their _____, _____, nationality, or sex.

5. Traditional tolerance _____, _____, and _____ the individual without the necessarily approving of or participating in his/her beliefs or behavior.

B. The New Tolerance.

To be truly tolerant, you must agree that _____ as your own. You must give your _____, your _____, your sincere _____ to their _____ and _____.

1. The new tolerance may sound like traditional tolerance, but it is vastly different.

   a. It is based on the belief that "truth is relative to the community in which a person participates. And since there are many human communities, there are necessarily many different truths."

   b. "Since truth is described by language, and all language is created by humans, all truth is created by humans."

   c. If all truth is created by humans, and all humans are "created equal," then all truth is equal.

2. In contrast to traditional tolerance, which asserts that everyone has an equal right to believe or say what he thinks is right, the new tolerance says that what every individual believes or says is _____, and _____.

(Josh McDowell. *The New Tolerance*. Tyndale Press, 1998)

THINKING

"Notice that one can't tolerate someone unless he disagrees with him. We don't "tolerate" people who share our views. They're on our side. There's nothing to put up with. Tolerance is reserved for those we think are wrong.

This essential element of tolerance--disagreement--has been completely lost in the modern distortion of the concept. Nowadays, if you think someone is wrong, you're called intolerant.

This presents us with a very curious problem. Judging someone wrong makes one intolerant, yet one must first think another is wrong in order to be tolerant. It's a "Catch-22." According to this approach, true tolerance is impossible."

Greg Koukl   www.str.org

II. The Cost of Tolerance:

The Bible makes it clear that all values, beliefs, lifestyles, and truth claims are not equally valid.

1. It teaches that the God of the Bible is the true God (Jeremiah 10:10)
2. All of His words are true (Psalm 119:160)

Chapter Fourteen - Tolerance

3. If something is not right in God's sight, it is wrong (Deut. 6:18).

4. Jesus is the only way to heaven (John 14:6)

Proponents of the <u>new tolerance</u> have no problem being intolerant to Christians, Christianity, and Christian morality because those things present problems for the new tolerance in four basic areas:

1. _____
2. _____
3. _____
4. _____

THINKING

Question: Is the way tolerance is being defined important when it is being used in newscast/articles?

Question: Was Jesus "tolerant" or "intolerant". How and why?

Question: Is it intolerant to call a certain action wrong or a "sin"?

Question: When a Christian tells others about salvation through Jesus is it implied that the other person's position/belief system is wrong? Is this "intolerant"?

III. Tolerance and the Christian.

The Bible makes it clear how Christians are to act toward each other and toward those outside of the faith:

a. Romans 12:16   b. Romans 12:18   c. Ephesians 4:2
d. Ephesians 4:32 e. Colossians 3:13 f. Galatians 6:10

In all this we must still stand up for and speak the TRUTH in love

I Peter 3:15-16 (NLT) *Instead, you must worship Christ as Lord of your life. And if you are asked about your Christian hope, always be ready to explain it. (16) But you must do this in a gentle and respectful way. Keep your conscience clear. Then if people speak evil against you, they will be ashamed when they see what a good life you live because you belong to Christ.*

Ephesians 4:14-15 (KJV) *That we [henceforth] be no more children, tossed to and fro, and carried about with every wind of doctrine, by the sleight of men, [and] cunning craftiness, whereby they lie in wait to deceive; (15) But speaking the truth in love, may grow up into him in all things, which is the head, [even] Christ:*

2 Timothy 2:24-26 (NLT) - *The Lord's servants must not quarrel but must be kind to everyone. They must be able to teach effectively and be patient with difficult people. 25They should gently teach those who oppose the truth. Perhaps God will change those people's hearts, and they will believe the truth. 26Then they will come to their senses and escape from the Devil's trap. For they have been held captive by him to do whatever he wants.*

Chapter Fourteen - Tolerance

Chapter Fourteen - Tolerance

BIBLIOGRAPHY

Beckwith, Francis J., and Gregory Koukl. *Relativism: Feet Firmly Planted in Mid-Air*. Grand Rapids: Baker Press, 2001.

Beckwith, Francis J., William Lane Craig, and J. P. Moreland, eds. *To Everyone An Answer: A Case for the Christian Worldview*. Downers Grove, Illinois: InterVarsity Press, 2004.

Beilby, James K. *Thinking About Christian Apologetics*. Downers Grove, Illinois: IVP Academic, 2011.

Benedict, Ruth. *Patterns of Culture*. 1934. Boston: Houghton Mifflin Company, 1989.

Bertrand, J. Mark. *(Re)Thinking Worldview: Learning to Think, Live, and Speak in This World*. Wheaton: Crossway Books, 2007.

Bruce, Tammy. *The Death of Right and Wrong*. Roseville, California: Prima Publishing, 2003.

Budziszewski, J. *Written On The Heart: The Case For Natural Law*. Downers Grove, Illinois: InterVarsity Press, 1997.

Chaffee, John. *Thinking Critically*. 6th ed. Boston: Houghton Mifflin Company, 2000.

Colson, Charles., and Nancy Pearcey. *How Shall We Then Live*. Wheaton: Tyndale House Publishers, 1999.

Copan, Paul and William Lane Craig, eds. *Contending With Christianity's Critics*. Nashville: B&H Academic, 2009.

Copan, Paul. *That's Just Your Interpretation: Responding To Skeptics Who Challenge Your Faith*. Grand Rapids: Baker Books, 2001.

_____. *When God Goes To Starbucks: A Guide To Everyday Apologetics*. Grand Rapids: Baker Books, 2008.

Coppenger, Mark. *Moral Apologetics for Contemporary Christians*. Nashville, Tennessee: B&H Publishing Group, 2011.

Corduan, Wnifried. *Pocket Guide to World Religions*. Downers Grove, Illinois: Inter-Varsity Press, 2006.

Craig, William Lane and Chad Meister. *God is Good God is Great: Why Believing in God is Reasonable and Responsible*. Downers Grove, Illinois: IVP Books, 2009.

Craig, William Lane. *Reasonable Faith: Christian Truth and Apologetics*. Wheaton, Illinois: Crossway Books, 2008.

Dawkins, Richard. *The God Delusion*. New York: Houghton Mifflin Company, 2006.

Dembski, William A. *The End of Christianity: Finding A Good God in an Evil World*. Nashville: B&H Publishing Group, 2009.

Dembski, William A. and Michael R. Licona, eds. *Evidence for God*. Grand Rapids: Baker Books, 2010.

Dockery, David S., ed. *Faith and Learning: A Handbook for Christian Higher Education*. Nashville, Tennessee: B&H Academic, 2012.

Dockery, David S and Timothy George, eds. *The Great Tradition of Christian Thinking: A Student's Guide*. Wheaton, Illinois: Crossway, 2012.

Fletcher, Joseph. *Situation Ethics*. Philadelphia: Westminster Press, 1966.

Gilbert, Greg. *What Is The Gospel?*. Wheaton, Illinois: Crossway, 2010.

Goheen, Michael, W. and Craig G. Bartholomew. *Living At The Crossroads: An Introduction to Christian Worldview*. Grand Rapids: Baker Academic, 2008.

Groothuis, Douglas. *Truth Decay: Defending Christianity Against the Challenges of Postmodernism*. Downers Grove, Illinois: InterVarsity Press, 2000.

_____. *Christian Apologetics: A Comprehensive Case for Biblical Faith*. Downers Grove, Illinois: IVP Academic, 2011.

Harris, Sam. *Letter to a Christian Nation*. New York: Vintage Books 2006.

Haught, John F. *God and the New Atheism: A Critical Response to Dawkins, Harris, and Hitchens*. Louisville: Westminster John Knox Press, 2008.

Hexham, Irving. *Understanding World Religions*. Grand Rapids: Zondervan, 2011.

Hibbs, Thomas S. *Shows About Nothing: Nihilism in Popular Culture from the Exorcist to Seinfeld*. Dallas: Spence Publishing Company, 1999.

Hiebert, Paul G. *Transforming Worldviews: An Anthropological Understanding of How People Change*. Grand Rapids: Baker Academic, 2008.

Hindson, Ed and Ergun Caner, eds. *The Popular Encyclopedia of Apologetics*. Eugene, Oregon: Harvest House Publishers, 2008.

Hoffecker, W. Andrew (ed). *Revolutions in Worldview: Understanding the Flow of Western Thought*. Phillipsburg, New Jersey: P&R Publishing, 2007.

Holmes, Arthur F. *Ethics: Approaching Moral Decisions*. Downers Grove, Illinois: IVP Academic, 2007.

Horner, David A. *Mind Your Faith*. Downers Grove, Illinois: IVP Academic, 2011.

House, H. Wayne and Dennis W. Jowers. *Reasons for Our Hope: An Introduction to Christian Apologetics*. Nashville, Tennessee: B&H Academic, 2011.

Huffman, Douglas S., ed. *Christian Contours: How a Biblical Worldview Shapes the Mind and Heart.* Grand Rapids, Michigan: Kregel Publications, 2011.

Keller, Timothy. *The Reason for God: Belief in an Age of Skepticism.* New York: Dutton, 2008.

Luther, Martin. Harold Grimm, ed. *Christian Liberty.* Philadelphia, PA: Fortress Press, 1957.

MacArthur, John. *Think Biblically: Recovering a Christian Worldview.* Wheaton, Illinois: Crossway Books, 2003.

Markos, Louis. *Apologetics for the 21st Century.* Wheaton, Illinois: Crossway, 2010.

McDowell, Josh. *The New Evidence That Demands A Verdict.* Nashville: Thomas Nelson, 1999.

McDowell, Josh and Bob Hostetler. *The New Tolerance: How a Cultural Movement Threatens to Destroy You, Your Faith, and Your Children.* Wheaton, Illinois: Tyndale House Publishers, 1998.

Mohler, R. Albert Jr. *Atheism Remix: A Christian Confronts the New Atheists.* Wheaton, Illinois: Crossway Books, 2008.

_____. *Culture Shift, Engaging Current Issues with Timeless Truth.* Colorado Springs, Colorado, Multnomah Books, 2008.

Moreland, J. P. *Love Your God with All Your Mind: The Role of Reason in the Life of the Soul.* Colorado Springs: NavPress, 1997.

Moreland, J. P. and William Lane Craig. *Philosophical Foundations for a Christian Worldview.* Downers Grove, Illinois: InterVarsity Press, 2003.

Morrow, Jonathan. *Think Christianly: Looking at the Intersection of Faith and Culture.* Grand Rapids, Michigan: Zondervan, 2011.

Noebel, David, A. *Understanding The Times.* Manitou Springs, Colorado: Summit Press, 2008.

Paul, Richard W. and Linda Elder. *Critical Thinking: Tools for Taking Charge of Your Professional and Personal Life.* Upper Saddle, New Jersey: Financial Times Prentice Hall, 2002.

Pearcey, Nancy. *Saving Leonardo: A Call to Resist the Secular Assault on Mind, Morals, and Meaning.* Nashville: B & H Publishing Group, 2010.

_____. *Total Truth: Liberating Christianity from Its Cultural Captivity.* Wheaton, Illinois: Crossway Books, 2004.

Piper, John and David Mathis, eds. *Thinking, Loving, Doing: A Call to Glorify God with Heart and Mind.* Wheaton, Illinois: Crossway, 2011.

Samples, Kenneth Richard. *A World of Difference: Putting Christian Truth-Claims to the Worldview Test*. Grand Rapids: Baker Books, 2007.

Sire, James W. *The Universe Next Door*. Downers Grove: Intervarsity Press, 5th edition, 2009.

Sproul, R. C. *The Consequences of Ideas: Understanding the Concepts That Shaped Our World*. Wheaton, Illinois: Crossway Books, 2000.

Stetson, Brad and Joseph G. Conti. *The Truth About Tolerance: Pluralism, Diversity and the Culture Wars*. Downers Grove, Illinois: InterVarsity Press, 2005.

Walsh, Brian J. & J. Richard Middleton. *The Transforming Vision: Shaping a Christian Worldview*. Downers Grove: Intervarsity Press, 1984.

Waxman, Trevin. *Counterfeit Gospels: Rediscovering the Good News in a World of False Hope*. Chicago, Illinois: Moody Publishers, 2011.

Weider, Lew and Ben Gutierrez. *Consider*. Virginia Beach, Virginia: Academx Publishing Services, 2011.

Wells, David F. *The Courage to be Protestant: Truth-lovers, Marketers, and Emergents in the Postmodern* World. Grand Rapids, Michigan: William B. Eerdmans, 2008.

Wolters, Albert M. *Creation Regained Biblical Basics for a Reformational Worldview*. Grand Rapids: Eerdmans Publishing, 1985.

Zacharias, Ravi and Norman Geisler, eds. *Who Made God?* Grand Rapids: Zondervan, 2003.